WAITING FOR GODOT

A Tragicomedy in Two Acts

by

SAMUEL BECKETT

SAMUEL  FRENCH

LONDON

NEW YORK TORONTO SYDNEY HOLLYWOOD

ISBN 0 573 04008 7

Please see page iv for further copyright information.

WAITING FOR GODOT

Produced at the Criterion Theatre, London, on the 12th September, 1955, with the following cast of characters:

(in the order of their appearance)

ESTRAGON	*Peter Woodthorpe*
VLADIMIR	*Hugh Burden*
LUCKY	*Timothy Bateson*
POZZO	*Peter Bull*
A BOY	*Michael Walker*

Directed by PETER HALL
Setting by PETER SNOW

SYNOPSIS OF SCENES

ACT I
A country road. Evening

ACT II
The same. The following evening

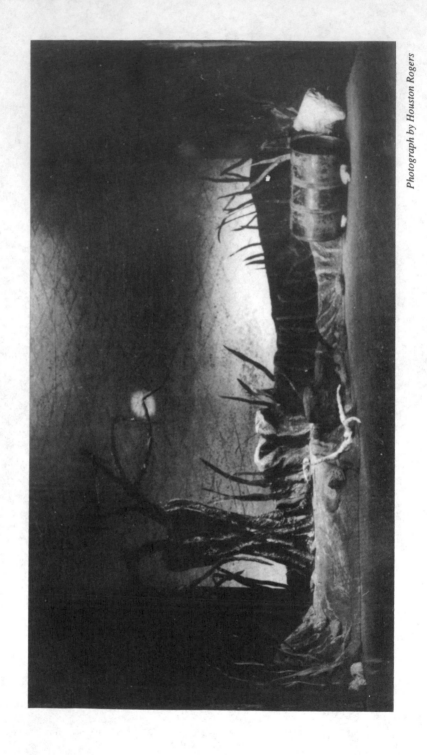

ACT I

SCENE—*A country road. Evening.*
A rostrum in the form of a bank or piece of high ground runs back stage from R *to* LC, *with a slope or ramp* R *leading down to stage level. The bank* LC *is shaped in the form of a low mound to serve as a seat. On the rostrum* C *is a leafless tree. There is a tree stump* C *and an empty tar barrel lies on its side* LC. *There are wings* R *and* L, *with exits up* R, *down* R, *and* L.
(See the Ground Plan and Photograph of the Scene)

When the CURTAIN *rises,* ESTRAGON *is seated on the mound, trying to remove one of his boots. He pulls at it with both hands, panting. He stops, exhausted, rests, tries again, but again fails.* VLADIMIR *enters up* R. *with short, stiff strides, his legs wide apart.*

ESTRAGON (*giving up*) Nothing to be done.
VLADIMIR (*crossing on the rostrum to* LC) I'm beginning to come round to that opinion. (*He turns, crosses and stands at the top of the ramp* RC) All my life I've tried to put it from me, saying, "Vladimir, be reasonable, you haven't yet tried everything." And I resumed the struggle. (*He broods, musing on the struggle. To Estragon*) So there you are.
ESTRAGON. Am I?
VLADIMIR. I'm glad to see you back. I thought you were gone for ever.
ESTRAGON. Me, too.
VLADIMIR. Together again at last. (*He moves down to the foot of the ramp,* R *of Estragon*) We'll have to celebrate this. But how? (*He reflects*) Get up till I embrace you.
ESTRAGON (*irritably*) Not now, not now.
VLADIMIR (*hurt; coldly*) May one enquire where his Highness spent the night?
ESTRAGON. In a ditch.
VLADIMIR (*admiringly*) A ditch! Where?
ESTRAGON (*without a gesture*) Over there.
VLADIMIR. And they didn't beat you?
ESTRAGON. Beat me? Certainly they beat me.
VLADIMIR. The same lot as usual?
ESTRAGON. The same? I don't know.
VLADIMIR. When I think of it—all these years—but for me— where would you be? (*Decisively*) You'd be nothing more than a little heap of bones at the present minute, no doubt about it.
ESTRAGON. And what of it?

VLADIMIR (*crossing below Estragon and standing down* L) It's too much for one man. (*He pauses. Cheerfully*) On the other hand what's the good of losing heart now, that's what I say. We should have thought of it when the world was young, in the nineties.

ESTRAGON. Ah, stop blathering and help me off with this bloody thing.

VLADIMIR. Hand in hand from the top of the Eiffel Tower, among the first. (*He pauses*) We were respectable in those days. Now it's too late. They wouldn't even let us up.

(ESTRAGON *tears at his boot*)

(*He moves to Estragon and puts a hand on his shoulder. After a pause*) What are you doing?

ESTRAGON. Taking off my boot. Did that never happen to you?

VLADIMIR. Boots must be taken off every day. I'm tired telling you that. Why don't you listen to me?

ESTRAGON (*feebly*) Help me!

VLADIMIR. It hurts?

ESTRAGON. Hurts! He wants to know if it hurts.

VLADIMIR (*moving to the barrel; angrily*) No-one ever suffers but you. I don't count. I'd like to hear what you'd say if you had what I have. (*He sits on the barrel*)

ESTRAGON. It hurts?

VLADIMIR. Hurts! He wants to know if it hurts.

ESTRAGON. What do you expect, you always wait till the last moment.

VLADIMIR (*musingly*) The last moment . . . (*He meditates*) Hope deferred maketh the something sick, who said that?

ESTRAGON. Why don't you help me?

VLADIMIR. Sometimes I feel it coming all the same. Then I go all queer. (*He takes off his hat, peers inside it, feels about inside it, shakes it, then replaces it on his head*) How shall I say? Relieved and at the same time—(*he searches for the word*) appalled. (*With emphasis*) Appalled. (*He takes off his hat and peers inside it*) Funny. (*He knocks on the crown as if to dislodge a foreign body, peers into it and replaces it on his head*) Nothing to be done.

(ESTRAGON, *with a supreme effort, succeeds in pulling off his boot. He looks inside it, feels about inside it, turns it upside down, shakes it, looks on the ground to see if anything has fallen out, finds nothing, feels inside it again, staring sightlessly before him*)

(*After a pause*) Well?

ESTRAGON. Nothing.

VLADIMIR. Show.

ESTRAGON. There's nothing to show.

VLADIMIR. Try and put it on again.

ESTRAGON (*having examined his foot*) I'll air it for a bit.

VLADIMIR. There's man all over for you, blaming on his boots the faults of his feet. (*He takes off his hat, looks inside it, feels about inside it, knocks on the crown, blows into it, then replaces it on his head*) This is getting alarming.

(*There is a silence.* VLADIMIR *is deep in thought.* ESTRAGON *pulls at his toes*)

(*Presently*) One of the thieves was saved. (*He pauses*) It's a reasonable percentage. (*He pauses*) Gogo.

ESTRAGON. What?

VLADIMIR. Suppose we repented.

ESTRAGON. Repented what?

VLADIMIR. Oh . . . (*He reflects*) We wouldn't have to go into the details.

ESTRAGON. Our being born?

(VLADIMIR *breaks into a hearty laugh which he immediately suppresses, his hand pressed to his stomach, his face contorted*)

VLADIMIR. One daren't even laugh any more.

ESTRAGON. Dreadful privation.

VLADIMIR. Merely smile. (*He smiles suddenly from ear to ear, keeps smiling for a moment, then ceases as suddenly*) It's not the same thing. Can't be helped. (*He pauses*) Gogo.

ESTRAGON (*irritably*) What is it?

VLADIMIR. Did you ever read the Bible?

ESTRAGON. The Bible . . . (*He reflects*) I must have taken a look at it.

VLADIMIR. Do you remember the Gospels?

ESTRAGON. I remember the maps of the Holy Land. Coloured, they were. Very pretty. The Dead Sea was pale blue. The very look of it made me thirsty. "There's where we'll go," I used to say, "there's where we'll go for our honeymoon. We'll swim. We'll be happy".

VLADIMIR. You should have been a poet.

ESTRAGON. I was. (*With a gesture towards his rags*) Isn't that obvious?

(*There is a silence*)

VLADIMIR (*presently*) Where was I? How's your foot?

ESTRAGON. Swelling visibly.

VLADIMIR. Ah, yes, the two thieves. (*He rises and moves to* L *of Estragon*) Do you remember the story?

ESTRAGON. No.

VLADIMIR. Shall I tell it to you?

ESTRAGON. No.

VLADIMIR. It'll pass the time. (*He pauses*) It was two thieves, crucified at the same time as our Saviour. One of them . . .

ESTRAGON. Our what?

VLADIMIR. Our Saviour. Two thieves. One is supposed to have been saved and the other—(*he searches for the contrary of saved*) damned.

ESTRAGON. Saved from what?

VLADIMIR. Hell.

ESTRAGON. I'm going. (*He does not move*)

VLADIMIR. And yet—(*he pauses*) how is it—this is not boring you, I hope—how is it that of the four evangelists only one speaks of a thief being saved? (*He moves slightly towards* C) The four of them were there—or thereabouts, and only one speaks of a thief being saved. (*He pauses*) Come on, Gogo, return the ball, can't you, once in a way?

ESTRAGON (*with exaggerated enthusiasm*) I find this really most extraordinarily interesting. (*He puts his boot on the small stump*)

VLADIMIR. One out of four. Of the other three two don't mention any thieves at all and the third says that both of them abused him.

ESTRAGON. Who?

VLADIMIR. What?

ESTRAGON. What's all this about? (*He pauses*) Abused who?

VLADIMIR. The Saviour.

ESTRAGON. Why?

VLADIMIR. Because he wouldn't save them.

ESTRAGON. From hell?

VLADIMIR. Imbecile! From death.

ESTRAGON. I thought you said from hell.

VLADIMIR. From death, from death.

ESTRAGON. Well, what about it?

VLADIMIR. Then the two of them must have been damned.

ESTRAGON. And why not?

VLADIMIR. But the other apostle says that one was saved.

ESTRAGON. Well? They don't agree and that's all there is to it.

VLADIMIR. But all four were there. And only one speaks of a thief being saved. Why believe him rather than the others?

ESTRAGON. Who believes him?

VLADIMIR. Everybody. It's the only version they know.

ESTRAGON. People are bloody ignorant apes. (*He rises painfully, limps to* R, *halts, gazes into the distance off, with his hand screening his eyes. He turns, crosses to* L, *and gazes off into the distance*)

(VLADIMIR *watches Estragon, then moves to the small stump, picks up the boot, and peers into it*)

VLADIMIR (*hastily throwing the boot down*) Pah! (*He spits*)

(ESTRAGON *moves* C *and stands with his back to the audience*)

ESTRAGON (*after a pause*) Charming spot. (*He turns and moves down* C) Inspiring prospects. (*He turns to Vladimir*) Let's go.

VLADIMIR. We can't.

ESTRAGON. Why not?

VLADIMIR (*annoyed*) We're waiting for Godot.

ESTRAGON. Ah! (*He pauses*) You're sure it was here?

VLADIMIR. What?

ESTRAGON. That we were to wait.

VLADIMIR. He said by the tree. (*He moves to the tree*)

(*They look at the tree*)

Do you see any others?

ESTRAGON. What is it?

VLADIMIR (*moving down* RC) I don't know. A willow.

ESTRAGON (L *of Vladimir*) Where are the leaves?

VLADIMIR. It must be dead.

ESTRAGON. No more weeping.

VLADIMIR. Or perhaps it's not the season.

ESTRAGON. Looks to me more like a bush.

VLADIMIR. A shrub.

ESTRAGON. A bush.

VLADIMIR. A . . . What are you insinuating? That we've come to the wrong place?

ESTRAGON. He should be here.

VLADIMIR. He didn't say for sure he'd come.

ESTRAGON. And if he doesn't come?

VLADIMIR. We'll come back tomorrow.

ESTRAGON. And then the day after tomorrow?

VLADIMIR. Possibly.

ESTRAGON. And so on.

VLADIMIR. The point is . . .

ESTRAGON. Until he comes.

VLADIMIR. You're merciless.

ESTRAGON. We came here yesterday.

VLADIMIR. Ah, no, there you're mistaken.

ESTRAGON. What did we do yesterday?

VLADIMIR. What did we do yesterday?

ESTRAGON. Yes.

VLADIMIR. Why . . . (*Angrily*) Nothing is certain when you're about.

ESTRAGON. In my opinion we were here.

VLADIMIR (*looking around*) You recognize the place?

ESTRAGON. I didn't say that.

VLADIMIR. Well?

ESTRAGON. That makes no difference.

VLADIMIR. All the same—that tree—(*he faces front*) that bog.

ESTRAGON (*after a pause*) You're sure it was this evening?

VLADIMIR. What?

ESTRAGON (*moving up* RC) That we were to wait.

VLADIMIR (*moving up* R) He said Saturday. (*He pauses*) I think.

ESTRAGON. You think.

VLADIMIR (*moving down* R) I must have made a note of it. (*He fumbles in his pockets, which are bursting with miscellaneous rubbish*)

ESTRAGON (*moving to* L *of Vladimir; very insidious*) But what Saturday? (*He moves* RC) And is it Saturday? Is it not rather Sunday? (*He pauses*) Or Monday? (*He pauses*) Or Friday?

VLADIMIR (*looking wildly about him, as though the date was inscribed in the landscape*) It's not possible.

ESTRAGON. Or Thursday?

VLADIMIR. What'll we do?

ESTRAGON (*moving* C) If he came yesterday and we weren't here you may be sure he won't come again today.

VLADIMIR (*with a step towards Estragon*) But you say we were here yesterday.

ESTRAGON (*after a pause*) I may be mistaken. (*He pauses*) Let's stop talking for a minute, do you mind?

VLADIMIR (*feebly*) All right.

(ESTRAGON *sits on the stump and falls asleep*)

(*He paces up* R, *turns and paces to* R *of Estragon*) Gogo! (*He moves behind Estragon*) Gogo! (*He moves up* L *of Estragon*) GoGo!

(ESTRAGON *wakes with a start*)

ESTRAGON (*restored to the horror of his situation*) I was asleep. (*Reproachfully*) Why will you never let me sleep? (*He rises and moves up* RC)

VLADIMIR. I felt lonely.

ESTRAGON (*moving to* R *of Vladimir*) I had a dream.

VLADIMIR. Don't tell me.

ESTRAGON. I dreamt that . . .

VLADIMIR (*moving to the barrel and sitting*) Don't tell me!

ESTRAGON (*with a gesture towards the universe*) This one is enough for you?

(*There is a short silence*)

It's not nice of you, Didi. Who am I to tell my private nightmares to if I can't tell them to you?

VLADIMIR. Let them remain private. You know I can't bear that.

ESTRAGON (*coldly*) There are times when I wonder if it wouldn't be better for us to part.

VLADIMIR. You wouldn't go far.

ESTRAGON (*moving to* R *of Vladimir*) That would be too bad, really too bad. (*He pauses*) Wouldn't it, Didi, be really too bad? (*He pauses*) When you think of the beauty of the way. (*He pauses*) And the goodness of the wayfarers. (*He pauses. Wheedling*) Wouldn't it, Didi?

VLADIMIR. Calm yourself, calm yourself.

ESTRAGON (*voluptuously*) Calm—calm . . . The English say

"cawm". (*He pauses*) You know the story of the Englishman
in a brothel?

VLADIMIR. Yes.

ESTRAGON. Tell it to me.

VLADIMIR. Ah, stop it!

ESTRAGON. An Englishman having drunk a little more than
usual proceeds to a brothel. The bawd asks him if he wants a
fair one, a dark one, or a red-haired one. Go on.

VLADIMIR (*abruptly*) Stop it!

(VLADIMIR *rises, crosses and exits hurriedly* R. ESTRAGON *follows
him and looks off* R, *making gestures like those of a spectator encouraging
a pugilist.*

VLADIMIR *re-enters* R, *brushes past Estragon and, with his head
bowed, crosses to the barrel and sits*)

ESTRAGON (*with a step towards Vladimir; gently*) You wanted to
speak to me? (*He pauses, then takes another step towards Vladimir*) You
had something to say to me? (*He pauses, then takes another step*)
Didi . . .

VLADIMIR (*without looking up*) I've nothing to say to you.

ESTRAGON (*with a step forward*) You're angry? (*He pauses and
again steps forward*) Forgive me. (*He pauses, moves to Vladimir and
puts a hand on his shoulder*) Come, Didi. (*He pauses*) Give me your
hand.

(VLADIMIR *looks up*)

Embrace me.

(VLADIMIR *softens, rises, and embraces Estragon*)

(*He recoils and moves* RC) You stink of garlic.

VLADIMIR. It's good for the kidneys.

(*There is a silence.* ESTRAGON *looks attentively at the tree*)

What do we do now?

ESTRAGON (*moving up* RC) We wait.

VLADIMIR. Yes, but while we wait.

ESTRAGON (*after a pause*) What about hanging ourselves?

VLADIMIR (*moving up* C) From that bough. I wouldn't trust it.

ESTRAGON. We can always try.

VLADIMIR (*after a pause*) Go ahead.

ESTRAGON. After you.

VLADIMIR. No, no, you first.

ESTRAGON. Why me?

VLADIMIR. You're lighter than me.

ESTRAGON. Just so.

VLADIMIR. I don't understand.

ESTRAGON. Use your intelligence, can't you?

(VLADIMIR *stands with his back to Estragon and faces the audience.
There is a silence*)

VLADIMIR (*finally*) I remain in the dark.

ESTRAGON. This is how it is. (*He reflects*) The bough—the
bough . . . (*Angrily*) Use your head, can't you?

VLADIMIR. You're my only hope.

ESTRAGON (*with an effort*) Gogo light—bough not break—Gogo
dead. Didi heavy—bough break—Didi alone. Whereas . . .

VLADIMIR. I hadn't thought of that.

ESTRAGON. If it hangs you it'll hang anything.

VLADIMIR. But am I heavier than you?

ESTRAGON. So you tell me. I don't know. There's an even
chance. Or nearly.

VLADIMIR. Well? What do we do?

(*There is a pause.* ESTRAGON *thinks*)

ESTRAGON (*moving down* RC) Don't let's do anything. It's safer.

VLADIMIR. Let's wait and see what he says.

ESTRAGON. Who?

VLADIMIR (*moving to* L *of Estragon*) Godot.

ESTRAGON. Good idea.

VLADIMIR. Let's wait till we know exactly how we stand.

ESTRAGON. On the other hand, it might be better to strike the
iron before it freezes.

VLADIMIR. I'm curious to hear what he has to offer. Then
we'll take it or leave it.

ESTRAGON. What exactly did we ask him to do for us?

VLADIMIR. Were you not there?

ESTRAGON. I can't have been listening.

VLADIMIR. Oh—nothing very definite.

ESTRAGON. A kind of prayer.

VLADIMIR. Precisely.

ESTRAGON. A vague supplication.

VLADIMIR. Exactly.

ESTRAGON. And what did he reply?

VLADIMIR. That he'd see.

ESTRAGON. That he couldn't promise anything.

VLADIMIR. That he'd have to think it over.

ESTRAGON. In the quiet of his home.

VLADIMIR. Consult his family.

ESTRAGON. His friends.

VLADIMIR. His agents.

ESTRAGON. His correspondents.

VLADIMIR. His books.

ESTRAGON. His bank account.

VLADIMIR. Before taking a decision.

ESTRAGON. It's the normal thing.

VLADIMIR. Is it not?

ESTRAGON. I think it is.
VLADIMIR. I think so, too.

(*There is a silence*)

ESTRAGON (*presently; anxiously*) And we?
VLADIMIR (*moving* L) I beg your pardon?
ESTRAGON. I said, "And we"?
VLADIMIR. I don't understand.
ESTRAGON (*moving to Vladimir*) Where do we come in?
VLADIMIR. Come in?
ESTRAGON. Take your time.
VLADIMIR. Come in? (*He pauses*) On our hands and knees.
ESTRAGON (*after a pause*) As bad as that?
VLADIMIR. Your worship wishes to assert his prerogatives?
ESTRAGON. We've no rights any more?

(VLADIMIR *laughs and immediately represses it, as before*)

VLADIMIR. You'd make me laugh, if it wasn't prohibited.
ESTRAGON. We've lost our rights?
VLADIMIR. We waived them.

(*There is a silence. They remain motionless, arms dangling, heads bowed, sagging at the knees*)

ESTRAGON (*feebly*) We're not tied? (*He pauses*) We're not . . .
VLADIMIR (*raising his hand*) Listen!

(*They listen, grotesquely rigid*)

ESTRAGON. I hear nothing.
VLADIMIR. Hsssst!

(*They huddle together and listen*)

Nor I.

(*They sigh with relief, relax and separate*)

ESTRAGON (*moving* L) You gave me a fright.
VLADIMIR. I thought it was he.
ESTRAGON. Who?
VLADIMIR. Godot.
ESTRAGON. Pah! The wind in the reeds.
VLADIMIR. I could have sworn I heard shouts.
ESTRAGON. And why would he shout?
VLADIMIR. At his horse.

(*There is a silence*)

ESTRAGON (*presently*) I'm hungry.
VLADIMIR. Do you want a carrot?
ESTRAGON. Is that all there is?
VLADIMIR (*moving to Estragon*) I might have some turnips.

ESTRAGON. Give me a carrot.

(VLADIMIR *rummages in his pockets, takes out a turnip and gives it to Estragon*)

(*He takes a bite out of the turnip. Angrily*) It's a turnip!

VLADIMIR. Oh, pardon! I could have sworn it was a carrot. (*He rummages in his pockets and finds nothing but turnips*) All that's turnips. (*He rummages*) You must have eaten the last. (*He rummages*) Wait, I have it. (*He brings out a carrot and gives it to Estragon*) There, dear fellow. (*He sits on the mound*)

(ESTRAGON *wipes the carrot on his sleeve and begins to eat it*)

Make it last, that's the end of them.

ESTRAGON (*chewing*) I asked you a question.

VLADIMIR. Ah.

ESTRAGON. Did you reply?

VLADIMIR. How's the carrot?

ESTRAGON. It's a carrot.

VLADIMIR. So much the better, so much the better. (*He pauses*) What was it you wanted to know?

ESTRAGON (*after a pause*) I've forgotten. (*He chews*) That's what annoys me. (*He looks appreciatively at the carrot and dangles it between his finger and thumb*) I'll never forget this carrot. (*He sucks the end of the carrot, meditatively*) Ah, yes, now I remember.

VLADIMIR. Well?

ESTRAGON (*with his mouth full; vacuously*) We're not tied.

VLADIMIR. I don't hear a word you're saying.

(ESTRAGON *chews his mouthful of carrot and swallows it*)

ESTRAGON. I'm asking you if we're tied.

VLADIMIR. Tied?

ESTRAGON. Ti-ed.

VLADIMIR. How do you mean—tied?

ESTRAGON. Down.

VLADIMIR. But to whom. By whom?

ESTRAGON. To your man.

VLADIMIR. To Godot? Tied to Godot? What an idea. No question of it. (*He pauses*) For the moment.

ESTRAGON (*after a pause*) His name is Godot? (*He moves to the barrel*)

VLADIMIR. I think so.

ESTRAGON (*sitting on the barrel*) Fancy that. (*He raises what remains of the carrot by the stub of leaf, and twirls it before his eyes*) Funny, the more you eat the worse it gets.

VLADIMIR. With me it's just the opposite.

ESTRAGON. In other words?

VLADIMIR. I get used to the muck as I go along.

ESTRAGON (*after prolonged reflection*) Is that the opposite?

VLADIMIR. Question of temperament.
ESTRAGON. Of character.
VLADIMIR. Nothing you can do about it.
ESTRAGON. No use struggling.
VLADIMIR. One is what one is.
ESTRAGON. No use wriggling.
VLADIMIR. The essential doesn't change.
ESTRAGON (*rising*) Nothing to be done. (*He moves up* L *of Vladimir and proffers the remains of the carrot to him*) Like to finish it?

(*A terrible cry is heard off* R. VLADIMIR *rises.* ESTRAGON *drops the carrot. They remain motionless for a few moments, then together make a sudden rush to* L. ESTRAGON *stops half-way, runs back, picks up the carrot, stuffs it in his pocket, then runs towards* VLADIMIR, *who waits for him.* ESTRAGON *stops again, runs back, picks up his boot, then runs to rejoin* VLADIMIR. *They huddle together, behind the barrel, with shoulders hunched, cringing away from the menace.*

     LUCKY *enters* R. *He is being driven by means of a rope passed round his neck, long enough to allow him to reach the centre of the stage before Pozzo appears.* LUCKY *carries a heavy bag, a folding stool, a picnic basket and a greatcoat*)

POZZO (*off*) On! (*He cracks his whip*)

(POZZO, *holding the end of the rope, enters* R. *He and* LUCKY *move across the stage.*

     LUCKY *passes below Vladimir and Estragon and exits* L. POZZO *sees Vladimir and Estragon and stops short. The rope tautens*)

(*He violently jerks the rope*) Back!

(*The sound of* LUCKY *falling with his baggage, is heard off.* VLADIMIR *and* ESTRAGON *turn and look off* L, *divided between the wish to go to Lucky's assistance and the fear of not minding their own business.* VLADIMIR *takes a step towards the exit* L. ESTRAGON *holds him back by the sleeves*)

VLADIMIR. Let me go.
ESTRAGON. Stay where you are.
POZZO (*moving* LC *and coiling his end of the rope*) Be careful! He's wicked.

(VLADIMIR *and* ESTRAGON *turn towards Pozzo*)

With strangers.
ESTRAGON (*moving* RC; *in an undertone*) Is that him?

(VLADIMIR *moves to* R *of Pozzo, looks at him, then returns to* L *of Estragon*)

VLADIMIR. Who?
ESTRAGON (*trying to remember the name*) Er . . .
VLADIMIR. Godot?

ESTRAGON. Yes.

POZZO. I present myself: Pozzo.

VLADIMIR (*to Estragon*) Not at all.

ESTRAGON (*crossing to R of Pozzo; timidly*) You're not Mr Godot, sir?

POZZO (*in a terrifying voice*) I am Pozzo. (*He pauses*) Pozzo. (*He pauses*) Does that name mean nothing to you? (*He pauses*) I say does that name mean nothing to you?

(VLADIMIR *and* ESTRAGON *look questioningly at each other*)

ESTRAGON (*pretending to search*) Bozzo—Bozzo . . .

VLADIMIR (*pretending to search*) Pozzo—Pozzo . . .

POZZO (*loudly*) Pppozzzo!

ESTRAGON. Ah! Pozzo—let me see—Pozzo . . .

VLADIMIR. Is it Pozzo or Bozzo?

ESTRAGON. Pozzo—no—I'm afraid I—no—I don't seem to . . .

(POZZO *advances threateningly on* ESTRAGON, *who crosses above Vladimir to R of him*)

VLADIMIR (*conciliating*) I once knew a family called Gozzo. The mother embroidered d'oylies.

ESTRAGON (*hastily*) We're not from these parts, sir.

POZZO. You are human beings none the less. (*He puts on his spectacles*) As far as one can see. (*He removes his spectacles*) Of the same species as myself. (*He bursts into an enormous laugh*) Of the same species as Pozzo. Made in God's image!

VLADIMIR (*after a pause*) Well, you see . . .

POZZO (*peremptorily*) Who is Godot?

ESTRAGON. Godot?

POZZO. You took me for Godot.

VLADIMIR. Oh, no, sir, not for an instant, sir.

POZZO. Who is he?

VLADIMIR. Oh, he's a—he's a kind of acquaintance.

ESTRAGON. Nothing of the kind, we hardly know him.

VLADIMIR. True—we don't know him very well—but all the same . . .

ESTRAGON. Personally I wouldn't even know him if I saw him.

POZZO (*crossing below Vladimir to Estragon*) You took me for him.

ESTRAGON (*recoiling to R*) That's to say—you understand—the dusk — the strain — waiting — I confess — I imagined — for a second . . .

POZZO. Waiting? So you were waiting for him?

(ESTRAGON *moves up* C)

VLADIMIR (*turning to Pozzo*) Well, you see . . .

POZZO. Here? On my land?

VLADIMIR. We didn't intend any harm.

ESTRAGON (*moving to L of Vladimir*) We meant well.

POZZO. The road is free to all.

VLADIMIR. That's how we looked at it.

POZZO. It's a disgrace. But there you are.

ESTRAGON. Nothing we can do about it.

POZZO (*with a magnanimous gesture*) Let's say no more about it. (*He jerks the rope and calls*) Up, pig! (*He pauses*) Every time he drops he falls asleep. (*He jerks the rope*) Up, hog!

(*The sound of* LUCKY *rising and picking up his baggage is heard off*)

(*He jerks the rope*) Back!

(VLADIMIR *and* ESTRAGON *sit on the mound.* LUCKY *enters backwards* L)

Stop!

(LUCKY *stops*)

Turn!

(LUCKY *turns*)

(*To Vladimir and Estragon. Affably*) Gentlemen, I am happy to have met you.

(VLADIMIR *and* ESTRAGON *look incredulously at Pozzo*)

Yes, yes, sincerely happy. (*He jerks the rope*) Closer!

(LUCKY *advances*)

Stop!

(LUCKY *stops*)

(*To Vladimir and Estragon*) Yes, the road seems long when one journeys all alone for—(*he consults his watch*) yes—(*he calculates*) yes—six hours, that's right, six hours on end, and never a soul in sight. (*To Lucky*) Coat!

(LUCKY *puts down the bag, moves to Pozzo, gives him the coat, then returns to his place and picks up the bag*)

(*He holds out the whip*) Hold that!

(LUCKY *advances and, both his hands being occupied, takes the whip in his mouth, then returns to his place*)

(*He struggles to don his coat*) Coat!

(LUCKY *puts down the bag, basket and stool, moves to Pozzo, helps him on with his coat, then returns to his place and picks up the bag, basket and stool*)

Touch of autumn in the air this evening. (*He buttons his coat, stoops, inspects himself, then straightens up*) Whip!

(LUCKY *advances.* POZZO *snatches the whip from Lucky's mouth.* LUCKY *resumes his place*)

B

Yes, gentlemen, I cannot go for long without the society of my likes. (*He puts on his glasses and looks at Vladimir and Estragon*) Even when the likeness is an imperfect one. (*He takes off his glasses*) Stool!

(LUCKY *puts down the bag and basket, crosses to* RC, *opens the stool, sets it down, then returns to his place and picks up the bag and basket*)

Closer! (*He sits on the stool*)

(LUCKY *moves to Pozzo*)

(*He places the butt of his whip against Lucky's chest and pushes*) Back!

(LUCKY *backs up* RC)

Farther!

(LUCKY *takes another step back*)

Stop!

(LUCKY *stops*)

(*To Vladimir and Estragon*) That is why, with your permission, I propose to dally with you a moment, before I venture any farther. (*To Lucky*) Basket!

(LUCKY *advances, hands the picnic basket to Pozzo, then returns up* RC)

The fresh air stimulates the jaded appetite. (*He opens the basket! takes out a piece of chicken, a piece of bread and a bottle of wine*) Basket,

(LUCKY *moves to Pozzo, takes the basket, then crosses and stands down* L)

Farther.

(LUCKY *takes a step back*)

He stinks. (*He raises the bottle*) Happy days! (*He drinks from the bottle, puts it down and eats*)

(*There is silence.* ESTRAGON *rises, moves to Pozzo and looks at the food.* VLADIMIR *rises, moves to Lucky, then signs to* ESTRAGON *who crosses to him. Cautiously at first, then more boldly, they begin to circle about* LUCKY, *inspecting him up and down.* POZZO *voraciously eats his chicken, throwing away the bones after having sucked them.* LUCKY *sags slowly, until bag and basket touch the ground, then straightens up with a start and begins to sag again, with the rhythm of one sleeping on his feet*)

ESTRAGON. What ails him?
VLADIMIR. I think he's tired.
ESTRAGON. Why doesn't he put down his bags?
VLADIMIR. How do I know?

(*They move close to Lucky*)

Careful!

ESTRAGON. Say something to him.

VLADIMIR. Look!

ESTRAGON. What?

VLADIMIR (*pointing*) His neck.

ESTRAGON (*looking at Lucky's neck*) I see nothing.

VLADIMIR. Here.

ESTRAGON (*peering at Lucky's neck*) Oh, I say.

VLADIMIR. A running sore.

ESTRAGON. It's the rope.

VLADIMIR. It's the rubbing.

ESTRAGON. It's inevitable.

VLADIMIR. It's the knot.

ESTRAGON. It's the chafing.

(*They resume their inspection of Lucky, and dwell on his face*)

VLADIMIR (*after a pause*) He's not bad looking.

ESTRAGON (*shrugging his shoulders; with a wry face*) Would you say so?

VLADIMIR. A trifle effeminate.

ESTRAGON (L *of Lucky*) Look at the slobber.

VLADIMIR (R *of Lucky*) It's inevitable.

ESTRAGON. Look at the slaver.

VLADIMIR. Perhaps he's a half-wit.

ESTRAGON. A cretin.

VLADIMIR (*looking closer*) It looks like a goitre.

ESTRAGON (*looking closer*) It's not certain.

VLADIMIR. He's panting.

ESTRAGON. It's inevitable.

VLADIMIR. And his eyes.

ESTRAGON. What about them?

VLADIMIR. Goggling out of his head.

ESTRAGON. Looks at his last gasp to me.

VLADIMIR. It's not certain. (*He pauses*) Ask him a question?

ESTRAGON. Would that be a good thing?

VLADIMIR. What do we risk?

ESTRAGON (*to Lucky; timidly*) Mister . . .

VLADIMIR. Louder.

ESTRAGON (*louder*) Mister . . .

POZZO. Leave him in peace. (*He finishes eating and wipes his mouth with the back of his hand*)

(VLADIMIR *and* ESTRAGON *turn to Pozzo*)

Can't you see he wants to rest. (*To Lucky*) Basket! (*He strikes a match and lights his pipe*)

(LUCKY *sees the chicken bones on the ground and stares greedily at them*)

(*As Lucky does not move he throws the match angrily away and jerks the rope*) Basket, pig!

  (Lucky *almost falls, recovers his senses, advances, puts the bottle in the basket, then kneels* c. Estragon *stares at the bones*)

(*He strikes another match and lights his pipe*) What can you expect, it's not his job. (*He pulls at his pipe and stretches out his legs*) Ah! That's better.

Estragon (*crossing to* L *of Pozzo; timidly*) Please, sir . . .

Pozzo. What is it, my good man?

Estragon. Er—you've finished with the—er—you don't need the—er—bones, sir?

Vladimir (*scandalized*) You couldn't have waited?

Pozzo. No, no, he does well to ask. Do I need the bones? (*He turns the bones over with the end of his whip*) No, personally I don't need them any more.

  (Estragon *takes a step towards the bones*)

But——

  (Estragon *stops short*)

—but in theory the bones go to the carrier. He is therefore the one to ask.

  (Estragon *turns hesitantly towards Lucky*)

Go on, go on, ask him. Don't be afraid, he'll tell you.

  (Estragon *turns to Lucky*)

Estragon. Mister—excuse me, Mister . . .

Pozzo (*to Lucky*) You're being spoken to, pig. Reply! (*To Estragon*) Try him again.

Estragon. Excuse me, Mister, the bones, will you be wanting the bones?

  (Lucky *looks long at Estragon*)

Pozzo (*in raptures*) Mister!

  (Lucky *bows his head*)

Reply! Do you want them or don't you?

  (Lucky *is silent*)

(*To Estragon*) They're yours.

  (Estragon *makes a dart at the bones, picks them up, sits on the mound and gnaws the bones.* Lucky *collapses on the ground*)

I don't like it. I've never known him refuse a bone before. (*He looks anxiously at Lucky*) Nice business it would be if he fell sick on me. (*He puffs at his pipe*)

VLADIMIR (*exploding*) It's a scandal. (*He snatches his hat from his head and throws it down*)

(*There is a silence.* ESTRAGON, *flabbergasted, stops gnawing, then looks at Pozzo and Vladimir in turn.* POZZO *is outwardly calm.* VLADIMIR *is embarrassed*)

POZZO (*to Vladimir*) Are you alluding to anything in particular?

VLADIMIR (*stuttering resolute*) To treat a man—(*he gestures towards Lucky*) like that—I think that—no—a human being—no—it's a scandal!

ESTRAGON (*not to be outdone*) A disgrace. (*He resumes his gnawing*)

POZZO. You are severe. (*To Vladimir*) How old are you? If it's not a rude question.

(VLADIMIR *is silent*)

Sixty? Seventy? (*To Estragon*) How old would you say he was?

ESTRAGON. Eleven.

POZZO. I am impertinent. (*He knocks out his pipe against the whip, and rises*) I must be getting on. Thank you for your society. (*He reflects*) Unless I smoke another pipe before I go. What do you say?

(ESTRAGON *and* VLADIMIR *are silent*)

Oh, I'm only a small smoker, a very small smoker, I'm not in the habit of smoking two pipes on top of the other, it makes—(*he puts his hand to his heart and sighs*) my heart go pit-a-pat. (*He pauses*) It's the nicotine, one absorbs it in spite of one's precautions. (*He sighs*) You know how it is.

(*There is a short silence*)

But perhaps you don't smoke? Yes? No? It's of no importance. (*He makes as if to resume his seat*)

(VLADIMIR *looks at Pozzo*)

But how am I to sit down now, without affectation, now that I have risen? Without appearing to—how shall I say—without appearing to falter? (*To Vladimir*) I beg your pardon?

(VLADIMIR *is silent*)

Perhaps you didn't speak?

(VLADIMIR *is silent*)

It's of no importance. Let me see . . . (*He reflects*)

ESTRAGON (*rising and moving down* C) Ah! That's better. (*He puts the bones in his pocket*)

VLADIMIR (*picking up his hat*) Let's go.

ESTRAGON. So soon?

POZZO. One moment. (*He jerks the rope*) Stool! (*He points with his whip*)

(LUCKY *rises, moves to the stool and moves it slightly* C)

More! (*He points* C) There!

(LUCKY *places the stool* C *then stands down* R)

(*He sits on the stool*) Done it. (*He fills his pipe*)

VLADIMIR. Let's get out of here.

POZZO. I hope I'm not driving you away. Wait a little longer, you'll never regret it.

ESTRAGON (*scenting charity*) We're in no hurry.

POZZO. He can no longer endure my presence. I am perhaps not particularly human, but who cares?

(VLADIMIR *turns to go*)

(*To Vladimir*) Think twice, before you do anything rash.

(VLADIMIR *stops, turns and moves to* L *of Pozzo.* ESTRAGON *moves to* R *of Pozzo*)

Suppose you go now, while it is still day, for there is no denying it is still day.

(VLADIMIR *and* ESTRAGON *look at each other*)

Good. What happens in that case—(*he takes the pipe from his mouth and examines it*) I'm out—(*he relights the pipe*) in that case—(*he puffs*) in that case—(*he puffs*) what happens in that case to your appointment with this Godet—Godot—Godin—anyhow you see who I mean, who has your future in his hands—(*he pauses*) at least your immediate future?

VLADIMIR. How did you know?

POZZO. He speaks to me again. If this goes on much longer we'll soon be old friends.

ESTRAGON. Why doesn't he put down his bags?

POZZO. I, too, would be happy to meet him. The more people I meet the happier I become. From the meanest creature one departs wiser, richer, more conscious of one's blessings. Even you —(*he looks ostentatiously in turn at them to make it clear they are both meant*) even you, who knows, will have added to my store.

ESTRAGON. Why doesn't he put down his bags?

POZZO. But that would astonish me.

VLADIMIR. You're being asked a question.

POZZO (*delighted*) A question. Who? What? A moment ago you were calling me "sir" in fear and trembling. Now you're asking me questions. No good will come of this.

VLADIMIR (*to Estragon*) I think he's listening.

ESTRAGON (*circling about Lucky*) What?

VLADIMIR. You can ask him now. He's on the alert.

ESTRAGON. Ask him what?

VLADIMIR. Why he doesn't put down his bags.

ESTRAGON. I wonder.

(POZZO *follows these exchanges with anxious attention, fearing lest the question get lost*)

VLADIMIR. Ask him, can't you.

POZZO (*to Vladimir*) You want to know why he doesn't put down his bags, as you call them.

VLADIMIR. That's it.

POZZO (*to Estragon*) You are sure you agree with that?

ESTRAGON. He's puffing like a walrus.

POZZO. The answer is this. (*To Estragon*) But stay still, I beg of you, you make me nervous.

VLADIMIR. Here.

ESTRAGON (*moving to* R *of Pozzo*) What is it?

VLADIMIR. He's about to speak.

(*They wait, motionless*)

POZZO. Good. Is everybody set? Is everybody looking at me? (*He looks at Lucky*) Will you look at me, pig!

(LUCKY *looks at Pozzo*)

Good. (*He puts his pipe in his pocket, takes out a little vaporizer and sprays his throat, puts the vaporizer in his pocket, clears his throat, spits, takes out the vaporizer again, sprays his throat, then replaces the vaporizer in his pocket*) I am ready. Is everybody listening? Is everybody ready? (*He looks at them all in turn, Lucky last of all, and jerks the rope*) Hog!

(LUCKY *raises his head*)

I don't like talking in a vacuum. Good. Let me see. (*He reflects*)

ESTRAGON (*crossing below the others to* L *of them*) I'm going.

POZZO. What was it exactly you wanted to know?

VLADIMIR. Why he . . . ?

POZZO (*angrily*) Don't interrupt me. (*He pauses. Calmer*) If we all speak at the same time we'll never get anywhere. (*He pauses*) What was I saying? (*He pauses. Louder*) What was I saying?

(VLADIMIR *mimics one carrying a heavy burden.* POZZO *looks at him, puzzled*)

ESTRAGON (*forcibly*) Bags! (*He points at Lucky*) Why? Always hold. (*He sags, panting*) Never put down. (*He opens his hands and straightens up with relief*) Why?

POZZO. Ah! Why couldn't you say so before? Why he doesn't make himself comfortable? Let's try and get it clear. Has he not the right to? Certainly he has. It follows that he doesn't want to. There's reasoning for you. And why doesn't he want to? (*He pauses*) Gentlemen, the reason is this.

VLADIMIR (*to Estragon*) Make a note of this.

Pozzo. He wants to impress me, so that I'll keep him.

Estragon. What?

Pozzo. Perhaps I haven't got it quite right. He wants to mollify me, so that I'll give up the idea of parting with him. (*He pauses*) No, that's not exactly it, either.

Vladimir. You want to get rid of him?

Pozzo. He imagines that when I see how well he carries I'll be tempted to keep him on in that capacity.

Estragon. You've had enough of him?

Pozzo. In reality he carries like a pig. It's not his job.

Vladimir. You want to get rid of him?

Pozzo. He imagines that when I see him indefatigable I'll regret my decision. Such is his miserable machination. As though I were short of slaves.

(*All three look at Lucky*)

Atlas, son of Jupiter!

(*There is a silence*)

Well, that's that. Any more questions?

Vladimir. You want to get rid of him?

Pozzo. Remark that I might have easily been in his shoes and he in mine. If chance had not willed otherwise. To each one his due.

Vladimir. You waagerrim?

Pozzo. I beg your pardon?

Vladimir. You want to get rid of him?

Pozzo. I do. But instead of driving him away as I might have done, I mean, instead of simply kicking him out on his backside, in the goodness of my heart I am bringing him to the fair, where I hope to get a good price for him. The truth is you can't drive such creatures away. The best thing would be to kill them.

(Lucky *weeps*)

Estragon. He's crying.

Pozzo. Old dogs have more dignity. (*He proffers his handkerchief to Estragon*) Comfort him, since you pity him.

(Estragon *hesitates*)

Come on.

(Estragon *crosses to* R *of Pozzo and takes the handkerchief*)

Wipe away his tears, he'll feel less forsaken.

(Estragon *hesitates*)

Vladimir (*crossing to Estragon*) Here, give it to me, I'll do it.

(Estragon, *with childish gestures, refuses to give the handkerchief to Vladimir*)

Pozzo. Make haste, before he stops.

(ESTRAGON *approaches Lucky and tries to wipe his eyes.* LUCKY *kicks him violently in the shins.* ESTRAGON *drops the handkerchief, recoils and staggers up* C, *howling with pain*)

(*To Lucky*) Hanky!

(LUCKY *puts down the bag and basket, picks up the handkerchief, gives it to Pozzo, then returns down* R *and picks up the bag and basket*)

ESTRAGON (*moving to the barrel*) Oh, the swine! (*He sits on the barrel and pulls up the leg of his trousers*) He's crippled me.

POZZO. I told you he didn't like strangers.

VLADIMIR (*sitting above Estragon on the barrel*) Shŏw.

(ESTRAGON *shows his leg*)

(*To Pozzo. Angrily*) He's bleeding.

POZZO. It's a good sign.

ESTRAGON. I'll never walk again.

VLADIMIR (*tenderly*) I'll carry you. (*He pauses*) If necessary.

POZZO. He's stopped crying. (*To Estragon*) You have replaced him as it were. (*Lyrically*) The tears of the world are a constant quantity. For each one who begins to weep, somewhere else another stops. The same is true of the laugh. (*He laughs*) Let us not then speak ill of our generation, it is not any unhappier than its predecessors. (*He pauses*) Let us not speak well of it, either. (*He pauses*) Let us not speak of it at all. (*He pauses*) It is true that the population has increased.

VLADIMIR (*to Estragon*) Try and walk.

(ESTRAGON *rises, limps to Lucky, spits on him, then moves and sits up* R *of Pozzo, on the mound*)

POZZO. Guess who taught me all these beautiful things. (*He pauses and points to Lucky*) My Lucky!

VLADIMIR (*looking at the sky*) Will night never come?

POZZO. But for him all my thoughts, all my feelings, would have been of common things. (*He pauses. With extraordinary vehemence*) Professional worries .(*Calmer*) Beauty, grace, truth of the first water, I knew they were all beyond me. So I took a stooge.

VLADIMIR (*startled from his inspection of the sky*) A stooge?

POZZO. Yes, a stooge. (*He pauses*) That was nearly sixty years ago. (*He consults his watch*) Yes, nearly sixty. (*He draws himself up proudly*) You wouldn't think it to look at me, would you?

(VLADIMIR *rises, crosses to* L *of Lucky and looks at him*)

Compared to him I look like a young man, no? (*He rises. After a pause*) Hat!

(LUCKY *puts down the basket and takes off his hat. His long white hair falls about his face. He puts his hat under his arm and picks up the basket*)

Now look. (*He takes off his hat, revealing that he is completely bald, then replaces his hat on his head*) Did you see?

VLADIMIR. And now you turn him away? Such an old and faithful servant.

ESTRAGON (*rising and moving to* L *of Pozzo*) Son of a bitch!

(POZZO *becomes more and more agitated*)

VLADIMIR. After having sucked all the good out of him you chuck him away like a—like a banana skin. Really . . .

(POZZO *crosses to* LC, *groans and clutches his head*)

POZZO. I can't bear it—any longer—the way he goes on—you've no idea—it's terrible—he must go. (*He brandishes his arms*) I'm going mad. (*He collapses, his head in his hands*) I can't bear it—any longer.

(*There is a silence. The others look at Pozzo.* LUCKY *shudders*)

VLADIMIR. He can't bear it.

ESTRAGON. Any longer.

VLADIMIR. He's going mad.

ESTRAGON. It's terrible.

VLADIMIR (*crossing to* L *of Lucky*) How dare you! It's abominable! Such a good master! Crucify him like that! After so many years! Really!

POZZO (*sobbing*) He used to be so kind—so helpful—and entertaining—my good angel—and now—he's killing me.

ESTRAGON (*to Vladimir*) Does he want to replace him?

VLADIMIR (*moving to the stool and sitting*) What?

ESTRAGON (L *of Vladimir*) Does he want someone to take his place or not?

VLADIMIR. I don't think so.

ESTRAGON. What?

VLADIMIR. I don't know.

ESTRAGON. Ask him.

POZZO (*moving to* L *of Estragon; calmer*) Gentlemen, I don't know what came over me. Forgive me. Forget all I said. (*More and more his old self*) I don't remember exactly what it was, but you may be sure there wasn't a word of truth in it. (*He draws himself up and strikes his chest*) Do I look like a man that can be made to suffer? Frankly? (*He rummages in his pockets*) What have I done with my pipe?

VLADIMIR. Charming evening we're having.

ESTRAGON. Unforgettable.

VLADIMIR. And it's not over.

ESTRAGON. Apparently not.

VLADIMIR. It's only beginning.

ESTRAGON. It's awful.

VLADIMIR. It's worse than being at the theatre.

ESTRAGON. The circus.

VLADIMIR. The music-hall.

ESTRAGON. The circus.

POZZO. What can I have done with that briar?

ESTRAGON. He's a scream. He's lost his dudeen. (*He laughs noisily*)

VLADIMIR (*rising*) I'll be back.

ESTRAGON. At the end of the corridor, on the left.

VLADIMIR (*putting his hat on the stool*) Keep my seat.

(VLADIMIR *crosses and exits* R)

POZZO (*sitting on the barrel*) I've lost my Dunhill.

ESTRAGON (*convulsed with merriment*) He'll be the death of me.

POZZO (*looking up*) You didn't by any chance see . . . (*He remarks the absence of Vladimir*) Oh! He's gone. Without saying good-bye. How could he? He might have waited.

ESTRAGON. He would have burst.

POZZO. Oh! (*He pauses*) Oh, well, then, of course in that case . . .

ESTRAGON (*moving* RC *and looking off* R) Come here.

POZZO. What for?

ESTRAGON. You'll see.

POZZO. You want me to get up?

ESTRAGON. Quick!

(POZZO *rises and moves to Estragon*)

Look!

(POZZO *puts on his glasses and looks off* R)

POZZO. Oh, I say!

ESTRAGON. It's all over.

(ESTRAGON *and* POZZO *move* LC.
VLADIMIR *enters sombrely* R. *He shoulders Lucky out of his way, kicks over the stool and paces agitatedly* RC)

POZZO. He's not pleased.

ESTRAGON (*to Vladimir*) You missed a treat. Pity.

(VLADIMIR *halts* C, *puts the stool on its feet and calms himself*)

POZZO. He subsides. (*He looks around*) All subsides. A great calm descends. Listen! (*He raises his hand*) Pan sleeps.

VLADIMIR. Will night never come?

(POZZO *stands* C, *with* ESTRAGON R *of him.* VLADIMIR *is* R *of Estragon. All three look at the sky*)

POZZO. You don't feel like going until it does?

ESTRAGON. Well, you see . . .

POZZO. Why, it's very natural, very natural. I, myself, in your situation, if I had an appointment with a Godin—Godet—Godot

—anyhow, you see who I mean, I'd wait till it was black night before I gave up. (*He looks at the stool*) I'd like very much to sit down, but I don't quite know how to set about it.

ESTRAGON (*crossing to* L *of Pozzo*) Could I be of any help?

POZZO. If you asked me, perhaps.

ESTRAGON. What?

POZZO. If you asked me to sit down.

ESTRAGON. Would that be a help?

POZZO. I fancy so.

ESTRAGON. Here we go. Be seated, sir, I beg of you.

POZZO. No, no, I wouldn't think of it. (*He pauses. Aside*) Ask me again.

ESTRAGON. Come, come, take a seat, I beseech you, you'll get pneumonia.

POZZO. You really think so?

ESTRAGON. Why, it's absolutely certain.

POZZO. You may be right. (*He sits on the stool*) Thank you, dear fellow. (*He consults his watch*) But I must really be getting along if I am to observe my schedule.

VLADIMIR. Time has stopped.

POZZO (*cuddling his watch to his ear*) Don't you believe it, sir, don't you believe it. (*He puts his watch in his pocket*) Whatever you like, but not that.

ESTRAGON (*to Pozzo*) Everything seems black to him today.

POZZO. Except the firmament. (*He laughs, pleased with his witticism*) But I see what it is, you are not from these parts, you don't yet know what our twilights can do. Shall I tell you?

(*There is a silence.* ESTRAGON *crosses, sits on the barrel and fiddles with his boot.* VLADIMIR *fiddles with his hat.* LUCKY's *hat falls unnoticed to the ground*)

I can't refuse you. (*He uses his vaporizer*) A little attention, if you please. What was I saying? Ah, yes, the night . . . (*He looks at the sky*) Look.

(*All look at the sky except* LUCKY, *who is dozing off again*)

(*He jerks the rope*) Will you look at the sky, pig!

(LUCKY *looks at the sky*)

Good. (*He pauses*) That's enough.

(*They stop looking at the sky*)

What is there so extraordinary about it? Qua sky? It is pale and luminous like any sky at this hour of the day. (*He pauses*) In these latitudes. (*He pauses*) When the weather is fine. (*Lyrically*) An hour ago—(*he looks at his watch; prosaically*) roughly—(*lyrically*) after having poured forth ever since—(*he hesitates; prosaically*) say ten o'clock in the morning—(*lyrically*) tirelessly torrents of red and white light, it began to lose its effulgence, to grow pale—(*he gives a gesture of the two hands lapsing by stages*) pale, ever a little paler, a little paler, until—(*he pauses dramatically, then gives an ample gesture of the two hands flung wide apart*) pppffff! Finished! It comes to rest. (*He pauses*) But—(*he raises his hand in admonition*) but —behind this veil of gentleness and peace—(*he raises his eyes to the sky*)——

(VLADIMIR *and* ESTRAGON *raise their eyes to the sky*)

—night is charging—(*vibrantly*) and will burst upon us—(*he snaps his fingers*) pop! Like that. (*His inspiration leaves him*) just when we least expect it. (*He pauses. Gloomily*) That's how it is on this bitch of an earth.

(*There is a long silence*)

ESTRAGON (*presently*) So long as one knows.
VLADIMIR. One can bide one's time.
ESTRAGON. One knows what to expect.
VLADIMIR. No further need to worry.
ESTRAGON. Simply wait.
VLADIMIR. We're used to it.
POZZO. How did you find me? ← *wants praise for his speech*

(VLADIMIR *and* ESTRAGON *look blankly at Pozzo*)

Good? Fair? Passable? Mediocre? Positively bad?
VLADIMIR (*first to understand*) Oh, very good, very, very good.
POZZO (*to Estragon*) And you, sir?
ESTRAGON. Oh, tray bong, tray, tray, tray bong.
POZZO (*fervently*) Bless you, gentlemen, bless you. (*He pauses*) I have such need of encouragement. (*He pauses*) I weakened a little towards the end, you didn't notice?
VLADIMIR. Oh, perhaps just a teeny weeny little bit.
ESTRAGON. I thought it was intentional.
POZZO. You see, my memory is defective.

(*There is a silence*)

ESTRAGON (*presently*) In the meantime, nothing happens.
POZZO. You find it tedious?
VLADIMIR. Somewhat.
POZZO (*to Estragon*) And you, sir?
ESTRAGON. I've been better entertained.

(*There is a silence.* POZZO *struggles inwardly*)

POZZO. Gentlemen, you have been—civil to me.
ESTRAGON. Not at all.
VLADIMIR. What an idea!
POZZO. Yes, yes, you have been correct. So that I ask myself is

there anything I can do in my turn for these honest fellows who
are having such a dull time.

ESTRAGON (*rising and moving to* L *of Pozzo*) Even a(bob)would be
welcome.

request is ignored.

shilling

VLADIMIR. We are not beggars.

POZZO. Is there anything I can do, that's what I ask myself, to
cheer them up. I have given them bones, I have talked to them
about this and that, I have explained the twilight, admittedly.
But is it enough, that's what tortures me, is it enough?

not noticed or just ignored?

ESTRAGON. Even sixpence.

VLADIMIR (*to Estragon; indignantly*) That's enough.

ESTRAGON. I couldn't accept less.

POZZO. Is it enough? No doubt. But I am liberal. It's my
nature. This evening. So much the worse for me. (*He jerks the rope*)

(LUCKY *looks at Pozzo*)

For I shall suffer, no doubt about that. (*He rises and picks up the
whip*) What do you prefer? Shall we have him dance, or sing, or
recite, or think, or . . .

ESTRAGON. Who?

POZZO. Who! You know how to think, you two?

VLADIMIR. He thinks?

POZZO. Certainly. Aloud. He even used to think very prettily
once, I could listen to him for hours. Now . . . (*He shudders*) So
much the worse for me. Well, would you like him to think something for us?

ESTRAGON. I'd rather he'd dance, it'd be more fun.

POZZO. Not necessarily.

ESTRAGON. Wouldn't it, Didi, be more fun?

VLADIMIR. I'd like well to hear him think.

ESTRAGON. Perhaps he could dance first and think afterwards,
if it isn't too much to ask him.

VLADIMIR (*to Pozzo*) Would that be possible?

POZZO. By all means, nothing simpler. It's the natural order.
(*He laughs briefly*)

VLADIMIR. Then let him dance.

(*There is a silence*)

POZZO (*to Lucky*) Do you hear, hog?

ESTRAGON. He never refuses.

POZZO (*after a pause*) He refused once. (*He pauses*) Dance,
misery!

(LUCKY *puts down the bag and basket, moves down* RC, *turns to
Pozzo and dances a few steps*)

ESTRAGON. Is that all?

POZZO. Encore!

(LUCKY *repeats the same movements*)

ESTRAGON. Pooh! I'd do as well myself. (*He imitates Lucky and almost falls*) With a little practice.

POZZO. He used to dance the farandole, the fling, the brawl, the jig, the fandango, and even the hornpipe. He capered. For joy. Now that's the best he can do. Do you know what he calls it? — dances.

ESTRAGON. The Scapegoat's Agony.

VLADIMIR. The Hard Stool. ——→ *lavatorial*

POZZO. The Net. He thinks he's entangled in a net.

VLADIMIR (*squirming like an aesthete*) There's something about it . . .

  (LUCKY *turns to pick up his burdens*)

POZZO (*as to a horse*) Whoa!

  (LUCKY *stiffens*)

ESTRAGON. Tell us about the time he refused.

POZZO. With pleasure, with pleasure. (*He fumbles in his pockets*) Wait. (*He fumbles*) What have I done with my spray? (*He fumbles*) Well, of all the . . . (*He looks up, consternation on his features. Faintly*) I can't find my pulverizer. — *vaporizer.*

ESTRAGON (*faintly*) My left lung is very weak. (*He coughs feebly. In ringing tones*) But my right lung is as sound as a bell.

POZZO (*in his normal voice*) No matter. What can't be cured must be endured. What was I saying? (*He ponders*) Wait. (*He ponders*) Well, I'll be . . . (*He raises his head*) Help me!

ESTRAGON. Wait!

VLADIMIR. Wait!

POZZO. Wait!

  (*All three simultaneously take off their hats, press their hands to their foreheads, and concentrate*) — take hats off to concentrate.

ESTRAGON (*triumphantly*) Ah!

VLADIMIR. He has it.

POZZO (*impatiently*) Well?

ESTRAGON. Why doesn't he put down his bags?

VLADIMIR. Rubbish!

POZZO. Are you sure?

VLADIMIR. Damn it, haven't you already told us?

POZZO. I've already told you?

ESTRAGON. He's already told you?

VLADIMIR. Anyway, he has put them down.

ESTRAGON (*with a glance at Lucky*) So he has. And what of it?

VLADIMIR. Since he has put down his bags it is impossible that we should have asked why he does not do so.

POZZO. Stoutly reasoned.

ESTRAGON. And why has he put them down?

POZZO. Answer us that.

VLADIMIR (*after a pause*) In order to dance.

one long time, the other weak? — ambiguity → ambiguous balance between the positive and negative.

ESTRAGON (*after a pause*)　True.
POZZO.　True.

(*There is a silence*)

ESTRAGON (*presently*)　Nothing happens, nobody comes, nobody
goes, it's awful.
VLADIMIR (*to Pozzo*)　Tell him to think.
POZZO.　Give him his hat.
VLADIMIR.　His hat?
POZZO.　He can't think without his hat.
VLADIMIR (*to Estragon*)　Give him his hat.
ESTRAGON.　Me! After what he did to me? Never!
VLADIMIR.　I'll give it to him. (*He does not move*)
ESTRAGON.　Tell him to go and fetch it.
POZZO.　It's better to give it to him.
VLADIMIR.　I'll give it to him. (*He moves, picks up the hat and
tenders it at arm's length to Lucky*)

(LUCKY *does not move*)

POZZO.　You must put it on his head.
ESTRAGON (*to Pozzo*)　Tell him to take it.
POZZO.　It's better to put it on his head.
VLADIMIR.　I'll put it on his head. (*He moves behind Lucky,
cautiously approaches him, puts the hat on Lucky's head and recoils
smartly* R)

(*There is a silence.* LUCKY *settles the hat on his head with his hand*)

ESTRAGON.　What's he waiting for?
POZZO.　Stand back.

(ESTRAGON *stands by the mound* C. VLADIMIR *stands* R. LUCKY
is LC)

(*He moves* LC *and jerks the rope*)　Think, pig!

(*There is a pause, then* LUCKY *begins to dance*)

Stop!

(LUCKY *stops*)

Forward!

(LUCKY *advances*)

Stop!

(LUCKY *stops*)

Think!

(*There is a silence*)

LUCKY (*presently*)　On the other hand with regard to . . .

hats off they take their to think.

 kicked him

Pozzo. Stop!

(LUCKY *stops speaking*)

Back!

(LUCKY *moves back*)

Stop!

(LUCKY *stops*)

Turn!

(LUCKY *turns and faces front*)

Think!

LUCKY. Given the existence as uttered forth in the public works of Puncher and Wattmann of a personal God quaquaquaqua with white beard——

(VLADIMIR *takes off his hat*)

——quaquaquaqua outside time without extension who from the heights of divine apathia divine athambia divine aphasia loves us dearly with some exceptions——

(POZZO *sits on the barrel*)

——for reasons unknown but time will tell and suffers like the divine Miranda with those who for reasons unknown but time will tell are plunged in torment plunged in fire whose fire and flames if that continues and who can doubt it will fire the firmament that is to say blast hell to heaven so blue still and calm so calm with a calm which even though intermittent is better than nothing but not so fast and considering what is more that as a result of the labours left unfinished crowned by the Acacacacademy of Anthropopopometry of Essy-in-Possy of Testew and Cunard it is established beyond all doubt all other doubt that that which clings to the labours of men that as a result of the labours unfinished of Testew and Cunard it is established as hereinafter but not so fast for reasons unknown that as a result of the public works of Puncher and Wattmann it is established beyond all doubt that in view of the labours of Popov and Belcher——

(ESTRAGON *sits on the stool*)

——left unfinished for reasons unknown of Testew and Cunard left unfinished it is established what many deny that man in Possy of Testew and Cunard that man in Essy that man in short that man in brief in spite of the progress of alimentation and defecation wastes and pines wastes and pines and concurrently simultaneously what is more for reasons unknown in spite of the strides of physical culture the practice of sports——

c

(VLADIMIR *crosses and stands up* L)

—such as tennis football running cycling swimming flying floating riding gliding conating camogie skating tennis of all kinds dying flying sports of all sorts autumn summer winter winter tennis of all kinds hockey of all sorts penicilline and succedanea in a word I resume and concurrently simultaneously for reasons unknown to shrink and dwindle in spite of the tennis I resume flying gliding golf over nine and eighteen holes tennis of all sorts in a word for reasons unknown in Feckham Peckham Fulham Clapham namely concurrently simultaneously what is more for reasons unknown but time will tell to dwindle dwindle I resume Fulham Clapham in a word the dead loss per capitem since the death of Samuel Johnson being to the tune of one inch four ounce per capitem approximately by and large more or less to the nearest decimal good measure round figures stark naked in the stockinged feet in Connemara in a word for reasons unknown no matter what matter the facts are there and considering what is more much more grave that it appears what is still more grave that in the light of the labours lost of Steinweg and Peterman it appears what is more much more grave that in the light the light the light of the labours lost of Steinweg and Peterman that in the plains in the mountains by the seas by the rivers running fire the air is the same and then the earth namely the air——

(ESTRAGON *rises and crosses to* R)

—and then the earth in the great cold the great dark the air and the earth abode of stones in the great cold alas alas in the year of their lord six hundred and something the air the earth the sea the earth abode of stones in the great deeps the great cold on sea on land and in the air I resume for reasons unknown in spite of the tennis the facts are there but time will tell I resume alas alas on on in short in fine on on abode of stones who can doubt it I resume but not so fast I resume the skull to shrink pine waste in spite of the tennis on on the beard the flames the tears the stones so blue so calm alas alas on on the skull the skull the skull the skull in Connemara in spite of the tennis the labours abandoned left unfinished graver still abode of stones in a word I resume alas alas abandoned unfinished the skull the skull in Connemara in spite of the tennis the skull alas the stones Cunard——

(*There is a general mêlée.* VLADIMIR *and* ESTRAGON *protest violently.* POZZO *jumps up and pulls on the rope. There is a general outcry.* ESTRAGON *moves to* R *of Lucky and seizes him.* VLADIMIR *moves to* L *of Lucky*)

—(*he pulls on the rope, staggers and shouts*) tennis—the stones—so calm—Cunard——

(*They all throw themselves on Lucky*)

POZZO. His hat!
LUCKY (*struggling and shouting*) —unfinished . . .

(VLADIMIR *seizes Lucky's hat.* LUCKY *becomes silent and falls to the ground. There is a pause during which the* victors *pant*)

ESTRAGON. Avenged!

(VLADIMIR *examines the hat and looks inside it*)

POZZO. Give me that. (*He snatches the hat from Vladimir, throws it on the ground and tramples on it*) There's an end to his thinking. ⊢—✱✱✱
VLADIMIR. But will he be able to walk?
POZZO. Walk or crawl. (*He kicks Lucky*) Up, pig!
ESTRAGON. Perhaps he's dead. (*He crosses to* L)
VLADIMIR (*crossing to* L) You'll kill him.
POZZO. Up, scum! (*He jerks the rope. To Vladimir and Estragon*) Help me!
VLADIMIR. How?
POZZO. Raise him up.

(VLADIMIR *and* ESTRAGON *cross to* LUCKY, *hoist him to his feet, support him for an instant, then let him go. He falls*)

ESTRAGON. He's doing it on purpose.
POZZO. You must hold him. (*He pauses*) Come on, come on, raise him up.
ESTRAGON. To hell with him!
VLADIMIR. Come on, once more.
ESTRAGON. What does he take us for?

(VLADIMIR *and* ESTRAGON *raise* LUCKY *and stagger with him down* R)

POZZO. Don't let him go.

(VLADIMIR *and* ESTRAGON *totter*)

Don't move. (*He fetches the bag and basket and takes them to Lucky*) Hold him tight. (*He puts the bag in Lucky's hand*)

(LUCKY *immediately drops the bag*)

Don't let him go. (*He picks up the bag and puts it in Lucky's hand*)

(LUCKY, *at the feel of the bag, gradually recovers his senses and his fingers finally close round the handle*)

Hold him tight. (*He puts the basket in Lucky's hand*)

(LUCKY *grips the basket*)

Now. You can let him go.

(VLADIMIR *and* ESTRAGON *move away from* LUCKY *who totters, reels, sags, but succeeds in remaining on his feet, bag and basket in his hands*)

(He picks up the whip and cracks it) Forward!

  *(*Lucky *takes a step towards the audience)*

Back!

  *(*Lucky *takes a step back)*

Turn!

  *(*Lucky *turns and faces* L)*

Done it! He can walk. *(He turns to Vladimir and Estragon)* Thank you, gentlemen, and let me—*(he fumbles in his pockets)* let me wish you—*(he fumbles)* wish you—*(he fumbles)* what have I done with my watch? *(He fumbles)* A genuine half-hunter, gentlemen, with deadbeat escapement. *(He sobs)* 'Twas my granpa gave it to me. *(He fumbles and searches on the ground)*

  *(*Vladimir *and* Estragon *search around)*

(He turns over the remains of Lucky's hat with his foot) Well, now, isn't that . . .

  *(*Vladimir *crawls through the barrel.* Estragon *searches up* R. Pozzo *is* RC *with* Lucky L *of him)*

Vladimir. Perhaps it's in your fob.
Pozzo. Wait. *(He doubles up in an attempt to apply his ear to his stomach and listens. After a pause)* I hear nothing.

  *(*Estragon *moves to* R *of Pozzo and* Vladimir *to* L *of him)*

Which of you smells so bad?
Estragon. He has stinking breath and I have stinking feet.
Pozzo. I must be getting along.

  (There is a silence)

Estragon. Then, adieu.
Pozzo. Adieu.
Vladimir. Adieu.
Estragon. Adieu.

  (There is a silence. No-one moves)

Vladimir. Adieu.
Pozzo. Adieu.
Estragon. Adieu.

  (There is a silence)

Pozzo. And thank you.
Vladimir. Thank *you.*
Pozzo. Not at all.
Estragon. Yes, yes.
Pozzo. No, no.

VLADIMIR. Yes, yes.
ESTRAGON. No, no. (*He moves and stands below the mound*)

(*There is a silence*)

POZZO. I don't seem to be able—(*he hesitates*) to depart.
ESTRAGON. Such is life.

(POZZO *turns and moves away from Lucky to* R, *paying out the rope as he goes*)

VLADIMIR (*moving and standing* L *of Estragon*) You're going the wrong way.
POZZO. I need a running start.

(POZZO, *paying out the rope to its end, exits* R)

(*Off. Calling*) Stand back! (*He cracks his whip*) On! On!
ESTRAGON. On! On!
VLADIMIR. On! On!

(POZZO, *off, cracks his whip.* LUCKY *moves towards the exit* L)

POZZO (*off*) Faster!

(POZZO *appears* R.
   LUCKY *exits* L. VLADIMIR *picks up the stool and hands it to Pozzo*)

(*He cracks his whip*) On! On!

(POZZO *exits* L. *As he goes,* VLADIMIR *and* ESTRAGON *take off their hats and wave their hands. There is a long silence*)

VLADIMIR (*presently*) That passed the time.
ESTRAGON. It would have passed in any case.
VLADIMIR. Yes, but not so rapidly.
ESTRAGON (*after a pause*) What do we do now?
VLADIMIR. I don't know.
ESTRAGON. Let's go.
VLADIMIR. We can't.
ESTRAGON. Why not?
VLADIMIR (*moving to the barrel and sitting*) We're waiting for Godot.
ESTRAGON. Ah!
VLADIMIR (*after a pause*) How they've changed.
ESTRAGON. Who?
VLADIMIR. Those two.
ESTRAGON. That's the idea, let's make a little conversation.
VLADIMIR. Haven't they?
ESTRAGON. What?
VLADIMIR. Changed.
ESTRAGON (*moving to the stump*) Very likely. They all change. (*He sits*) Only we can't.
VLADIMIR. Likely! It's certain. Didn't you see them?

ESTRAGON. I suppose I did. But I don't know them.
VLADIMIR. Yes, you do know them.
ESTRAGON. No, I don't know them.
VLADIMIR. We know them, I tell you. You forget everything. (*He pauses. To himself*) Unless they're not the same . . .
ESTRAGON. Why didn't they recognize us, then?
VLADIMIR. That means nothing. I, too, pretended not to recognize them. (*He pauses*) And then nobody ever recognizes us.
ESTRAGON. Forget it. (*He rises*) What we need . . . (*He takes a step* L) Ow!

(VLADIMIR *does not react*)

Ow!
VLADIMIR (*to himself*) Unless they're not the same . . .
ESTRAGON. Didi! It's the other foot. (*He hobbles towards the mound*)
VLADIMIR. Unless they're not the same . . .
BOY (*off* R; *calling*) Mister!

(ESTRAGON *halts. He and* VLADIMIR *look off* R)

ESTRAGON. Off we go again.
VLADIMIR (*calling*) Approach, my child.

(*The* BOY *enters timidly up* R *and stands up* C)

BOY. Mister Albert . . . ?
VLADIMIR. Yes.
ESTRAGON. What do you want?
VLADIMIR. Approach.

(*The* BOY *does not move*)

ESTRAGON (*forcibly*) Approach when you're told, can't you?

(*The* BOY *moves timidly down* C *a little*)

VLADIMIR. What is it?
BOY. Mr Godot . . . (*He breaks off*)
VLADIMIR. Obviously. (*He pauses*) Approach.

(*The* BOY *does not move*)

ESTRAGON (*violently*) Will you approach!

(*The* BOY *moves timidly to* R *of Vladimir*)

(*He moves to* R *of the Boy*) What kept you so late?
VLADIMIR. You have a message from Mr Godot?
BOY. Yes, sir.
VLADIMIR. Well, what is it?
ESTRAGON. What kept you so late?

(*The* BOY *looks at them in turn, not knowing to which he should reply*)

VLADIMIR (*to Estragon*) Let him alone.

ESTRAGON. You let me alone! (*To the Boy*) Do you know what time it is?

BOY (*recoiling*) It's not my fault, sir.

ESTRAGON. And whose is it? Mine?

BOY. I was afraid, sir.

ESTRAGON. Afraid of what? Of us? (*He pauses*) Answer me.

VLADIMIR (*rising*) I know what it is, he was afraid of the others.

ESTRAGON. How long have you been here?

BOY. A good while, sir.

VLADIMIR. You were afraid of the whip.

BOY. Yes, sir.

VLADIMIR. The roars.

BOY. Yes, sir.

VLADIMIR. The two other men.

BOY. Yes, sir.

VLADIMIR. Do you know them?

BOY. No, sir.

VLADIMIR. Are you a native of these parts? (*He pauses*) Do you belong to these parts?

BOY. Yes, sir.

ESTRAGON. That's all a pack of lies. (*He shakes the boy by the arm*) Tell us the truth.

BOY (*trembling*) But it is the truth, sir.

VLADIMIR. Will you let him alone! What's the matter with you?

(ESTRAGON *releases the Boy, moves* R *and covers his face with his hand.* VLADIMIR *and the* BOY *observe him.* ESTRAGON *drops his hand. His face is convulsed*)

What's the matter with you?

ESTRAGON. I'm unhappy.

VLADIMIR. Not really. Since when?

ESTRAGON. I'd forgotten.

VLADIMIR. Extraordinary the tricks that memory plays.

(ESTRAGON *tries to speak, renounces, limps to the mound, sits and begins to take off his boot*)

(*To the Boy*) Well? (*He sits on the barrel*)

BOY. Mr Godot . . . (*He hesitates*)

VLADIMIR. I've seen you before, haven't I?

BOY. I don't know, sir.

VLADIMIR (*after a pause*) You don't know me?

BOY. No, sir.

VLADIMIR. It wasn't you came yesterday?

BOY. No, sir.

VLADIMIR. This is your first time?

BOY. Yes, sir.

(*There is a silence*)

VLADIMIR. Words, words. (*He pauses*) Speak.

BOY (*in a rush*) Mr Godot told me to tell you he won't come this evening but surely tomorrow.

VLADIMIR (*after a pause*) Is that all?

BOY. Yes, sir.

VLADIMIR. You work for Mr Godot?

BOY. Yes, sir.

VLADIMIR. What do you do?

BOY. I mind the goats, sir.

VLADIMIR. Is he good to you?

BOY. Yes, sir.

VLADIMIR. He doesn't beat you?

BOY. No, sir, not me.

VLADIMIR. Whom does he beat?

BOY. He beats my brother, sir.

VLADIMIR. Ah, you have a brother?

BOY. Yes, sir.

VLADIMIR. What does he do?

BOY. He minds the sheep, sir.

VLADIMIR (*after a pause*) And why doesn't he beat you?

BOY. I don't know, sir.

VLADIMIR. He must be fond of you.

BOY. I don't know, sir.

VLADIMIR. Does he give you enough to eat?

(*The* BOY *hesitates*)

Does he feed you well?

BOY. Fairly well, sir.

VLADIMIR. You're not unhappy?

(*The* BOY *hesitates*)

Do you hear me?

BOY. Yes, sir.

VLADIMIR. Well?

BOY. I don't know, sir.

VLADIMIR. You don't know if you're unhappy or not?

BOY. No, sir.

VLADIMIR. You're like myself. (*He pauses*) Where do you sleep?

BOY. In the loft, sir.

VLADIMIR (*after a pause*) With your brother?

BOY. Yes, sir.

VLADIMIR. In the hay?

BOY. Yes, sir.

(*There is a silence*)

VLADIMIR (*presently*) All right, you may go.

BOY. What am I to say to Mr Godot, sir?

VLADIMIR. Tell him—(*he hesitates*) tell him you saw us. (*He pauses*) You did see us, didn't you?

BOY. Yes, sir.

(*The Boy steps back, hesitates, turns, then runs off up* R. *The light suddenly fails. In a moment it is night. The moon rises at the back, mounts in the sky and stands still, shedding a pale light on the scene*)

VLADIMIR. At last!) — *relieved*.

(ESTRAGON *rises and goes towards Vladimir, with a boot in each hand. He puts the boots on the ground* C, *then straightens up and contemplates the moon*)

What are you doing?

ESTRAGON. Pale for weariness.

VLADIMIR. Eh?

ESTRAGON. Of climbing heaven and gazing on the likes of us.

VLADIMIR. Your boots. What are you doing with your boots?

ESTRAGON (*looking at his boots*) I'm leaving them there. (*He pauses*) Another will come, just as—as—as me, but with smaller feet, and they'll make him happy.

VLADIMIR. But you can't go barefoot.

ESTRAGON. Christ did.

VLADIMIR. Christ! What's Christ got to do with it? You're not going to compare yourself to Christ!

ESTRAGON. All my life I've compared myself to him.

VLADIMIR. But where he was it was warm, it was dry.

ESTRAGON. Yes. And they crucified quick.

at the beginning Estragon had v. little Biblical knowledge.

(*There is a silence*)

VLADIMIR (*rising and moving to* L *of Estragon*) We've nothing more to do here.

ESTRAGON. Nor anywhere else.

VLADIMIR. Ah, Gogo, don't go on like that. Tomorrow everything will be better.

ESTRAGON. How do you make that out?

VLADIMIR. Did you not hear what the child said?

ESTRAGON. No.

VLADIMIR. He said that Godot was sure to come tomorrow. (*He pauses*) What do you say to that?

ESTRAGON. Then all we have to do is to wait on here.

VLADIMIR. Are you mad? We must take cover. (*He takes Estragon by the arm*) Come on.

(VLADIMIR *draws* ESTRAGON *up* R. ESTRAGON *yields, then resists. They halt up* R)

ESTRAGON (*looking at the tree*) Pity we haven't got a bit of rope.

VLADIMIR. Come on. It's getting cold. (*He draws Estragon up* C)

ESTRAGON. Remind me to bring a bit of rope tomorrow.

VLADIMIR. Yes, yes. Come on. (*He draws Estragon up* LC)

ESTRAGON. How long have we been together all the time, now?

VLADIMIR. I don't know. Fifty years perhaps.

ESTRAGON. Do you remember the day I threw myself into the Rhône?

VLADIMIR. We were grape harvesting.

ESTRAGON. You fished me out.

VLADIMIR. That's all dead and buried.

ESTRAGON. My clothes dried in the sun.

VLADIMIR. There's no good harking back on that. Come on. (*He draws Estragon up* L)

ESTRAGON. Wait.

VLADIMIR. I'm cold.

ESTRAGON. Wait! (*He moves to the mound*) I wonder if we wouldn't have been better off alone, each one for himself. (*He sits on the mound*) We weren't made for the same road.

VLADIMIR (*after a pause; without anger*) It's not certain.

ESTRAGON. No, nothing is certain.

(VLADIMIR *moves slowly and sits* L *of Estragon on the mound*)

VLADIMIR (*after a pause*) We can still part, if you think it would be better.

ESTRAGON. It's too late now.

(*There is a silence*)

VLADIMIR. Yes, it's too late now.

(*There is a silence*)

ESTRAGON. Well, shall we go?

VLADIMIR. Yes, let's go.

They do not move. *There is a pause, then—*

the CURTAIN *quickly falls*

[handwritten annotations at top: "tape? → indicative of repetitive process. → passing of time." and "place and time of day th same."]

ACT II

SCENE—*The same. The following day, the same time.*

When the CURTAIN *rises, Estragon's boots are on the ground down* C, *with the heels together and the toes splayed. Lucky's hat is near the mound. The tree has four or five leaves.* VLADIMIR *emerges from the barrel and stands erect. He looks long at the tree, then suddenly begins to move feverishly about the stage, up and down, back and forth. He halts before the boots, picks one up, examines it, sniffs it, manifests disgust, then puts it carefully back in its place. He paces* R *and gazes into the distance off, shading his eyes with his hand. He turns, paces* L, *and again gazes into the distance off, shading his eyes with his hand. He turns, moves* C, *halts suddenly, faces the audience and sings loudly in too high a key.*

VLADIMIR (*singing*)   *[handwritten: exaggerated.]*

> A dog came in . . .

(*Having begun too high he stops, clears his throat and resumes*)

> A dog came in the kitchen
> And stole a crust of bread.
> Then cook up with a ladle
> And beat him till he was dead.
>
> Then all the dogs came running
> And dug the dog a tomb . . .

(*He breaks off, broods a moment, then resumes*)

> Then all the dogs came running
> And dug the dog a tomb
> And wrote upon the tombstone
> For the eyes of dogs to come:
>
> A dog came in the kitchen
> And stole a crust of bread.
> Then cook up with a ladle
> And beat him till he was dead.
>
> Then all the dogs came running
> And dug the dog a tomb . . .

(*He breaks off, broods a moment, then resumes*)

> Then all the dogs came running
> And dug the dog a tomb . . .

[handwritten annotation at right: "stops in the same place."]

(He breaks off, broods a moment, then resumes softly)

And dug the dog a tomb . . .

(He remains a moment, silent and motionless, then begins to move feverishly about the stage. He halts again before the tree, comes and goes, before the boots, comes and goes, moves R, gazes into the distance, turns, crosses to L, gazes into the distance, then moves C and faces front)

> *(ESTRAGON enters L and crosses slowly to L of Vladimir. He is barefooted and his head is bowed. VLADIMIR turns and sees him)*

You again!

> *(ESTRAGON halts LC, but does not raise his head)*

(He moves to R of Estragon) Come here till I embrace you.

ESTRAGON. Don't touch me!

> *(VLADIMIR holds back, pained)*

VLADIMIR. Do you want me to go away? *(He pauses)* Gogo. *(He pauses and looks attentively at Estragon)* Did they beat you? *(He pauses)* Gogo!

> *(ESTRAGON remains silent, with his head bowed)*

Where did you spend the night?

ESTRAGON. Don't touch me. Don't question me. Don't speak to me.

> *(VLADIMIR moves C)*

Stay with me.

VLADIMIR. Did I ever leave you?

ESTRAGON. You let me go. *(He bows his head)*

VLADIMIR. Look at me.

> *(ESTRAGON turns his head away)*

(Violently) Will you look at me!

> *(ESTRAGON raises his head. They look long at each other, recoiling, advancing, their heads on one side, as before a work of art, trembling towards each other more and more, then they suddenly embrace, clapping each other on the back. VLADIMIR releases himself. ESTRAGON no longer supported, almost falls)*

ESTRAGON. What a day!

VLADIMIR. Who beat you? Tell me.

ESTRAGON. Another day done with.

VLADIMIR. Not yet.

ESTRAGON. For me it's over and done with, no matter what happens. *(He pauses)* I heard you singing.

VLADIMIR. That's right, I remember.

ESTRAGON. That finished me. I said to myself, he's all alone, he thinks I'm gone for ever, and he sings.

VLADIMIR. One isn't master of one's moods. All day I've felt in great form. (*He pauses*) I didn't get up in the night, not once.

ESTRAGON (*sadly*) You see, you do it better when I'm not there.

VLADIMIR. I missed you—and at the same time I was happy. Isn't that a queer thing?

ESTRAGON (*shocked*) Happy?

VLADIMIR. Perhaps it's not the right word.

ESTRAGON. And now?

VLADIMIR. Now? (*Joyously*) There you are again.

(ESTRAGON *laughs*)

(*Indifferently*) There we are again. (*Gloomily*) There I am again. (*He moves* R)

ESTRAGON. You see, you feel worse when I'm with you. I feel better alone, too.

VLADIMIR (*piqued*) Then why do you come crawling back?

ESTRAGON. I don't know.

VLADIMIR. No, but I do. It's because you don't know how to take care of yourself. I wouldn't have let them beat you.

ESTRAGON. You couldn't have stopped them.

VLADIMIR. Why not?

ESTRAGON. There were ten of them.

VLADIMIR. No, I mean before they beat you. I would have stopped you from doing whatever it was you were doing.

ESTRAGON. I wasn't doing anything.

VLADIMIR. Then why did they beat you?

ESTRAGON. I don't know.

VLADIMIR (*moving to* R *of Estragon*) Ah no, Gogo, the truth is there are things escape you that don't escape me. You must feel it yourself.

ESTRAGON. I tell you I wasn't doing anything.

VLADIMIR. Perhaps you weren't. But it's the way of doing it that counts, the way of doing it, if you want to go on living.

ESTRAGON (*facing front*) I wasn't doing anything.

VLADIMIR. You must be happy, too, deep down, if you only knew it.

ESTRAGON. Happy about what?

VLADIMIR. To be back with me again.

ESTRAGON. Would you say so?

VLADIMIR. Say you are, even if it's not true.

ESTRAGON. What am I to say?

VLADIMIR. Say, "I am happy".

ESTRAGON. I am happy.

VLADIMIR. So am I.

ESTRAGON. So am I.

VLADIMIR. We are happy.

ESTRAGON. We are happy. (*He pauses*) What do we do now, now that we're happy? (*He moves to the barrel*)

VLADIMIR. Wait for Godot. *— nothing has changed*

(ESTRAGON *sits on the barrel and groans. There is a silence, during which* VLADIMIR *moves up* R *and crosses to* L *of the tree*)

Things have changed here since yesterday.
ESTRAGON. And if he doesn't come?
VLADIMIR (*after a moment's incomprehension*) We'll see when the time comes. (*He pauses*) I was saying that things have changed here since yesterday.
ESTRAGON. Everything oozes.
VLADIMIR. Look at the tree.
ESTRAGON. It's never the same pus from one second to the next.
VLADIMIR. The tree, look at the tree.

(ESTRAGON *looks at the tree*)

ESTRAGON. Was it not there yesterday?
VLADIMIR. Yes, of course it was there. Do you not remember? We nearly hanged ourselves from it. But you wouldn't. Do you not remember?
ESTRAGON (*rising*) You dreamt it.
VLADIMIR. Is it possible that you've forgotten already?
ESTRAGON (*crossing to* RC) That's the way I am. Either I forget immediately or I never forget.
VLADIMIR. And Pozzo and Lucky, have you forgotten them, too?
ESTRAGON. Pozzo and Lucky?
VLADIMIR (*after a pause*) He's forgotten everything.
ESTRAGON (*moving up* RC) I remember a lunatic who kicked the shins off me. Then he played the fool.
VLADIMIR (*moving to* L *of Estragon*) That was Lucky.
ESTRAGON. I remember that. But when was it?
VLADIMIR. And his keeper, do you not remember him?
ESTRAGON. He gave me a bone.
VLADIMIR. That was Pozzo.
ESTRAGON. And all that was yesterday, you say?
VLADIMIR. Yes, of course, it was yesterday.
ESTRAGON. And here, where we are now?
VLADIMIR. Where else do you think? Do you not recognize the place?
ESTRAGON (*suddenly furious*) Recognize! (*He moves down* RC) What is there to recognize? All my lousy life I've crawled about in the mud. And you talk to me about scenery. (*He looks wildly about him and moves up* LC) Look at this muckheap! I've never stirred from it.
VLADIMIR. Calm yourself, calm yourself.
ESTRAGON (*turning to Vladimir*) You and your landscape. Tell me about the worms.

we are all going to die.

VLADIMIR. All the same, you can't tell me that this—(*he gestures*) bears any resemblance to—(*he hesitates*) to the Macon country, for example. You can't deny there's a big difference.

ESTRAGON. The Macon country! Who's talking to you about the Macon country?

VLADIMIR. But you were there yourself, in the Macon country.

ESTRAGON. No, I was never in the Macon country. I've puked my puke of a life away here, I tell you. Here! In the—(*he moves down* L) Cackon country. — play on Macon.

VLADIMIR (*moving to* R *of Estragon*) But we were there together, I could swear to it. Picking grapes for a man called ... (*He snaps his fingers*) Can't think of the name of the man, at a place called ... (*He snaps his fingers*) Can't think of the name of the place, do you not remember?

ESTRAGON (*calmer*) It's possible. I didn't notice anything.

red soil in Macon

VLADIMIR. But down there everything is red.

ESTRAGON (*exasperated*) I didn't notice anything, I tell you.

(*There is a pause.* VLADIMIR *sighs deeply, then sits on the mound*)

VLADIMIR. You're a hard man to get on with, Gogo.

ESTRAGON. It would be better if we parted.

VLADIMIR. You always say that, and you always come crawling back.

ESTRAGON. The best thing would be to kill me—(*he pauses*) like the other.

VLADIMIR. What other? (*He pauses and rises*) What other?

ESTRAGON. Like billions of others.

VLADIMIR (*sententiously*) To every man his little cross. (*He sighs and sits on the mound*) Till he dies. (*As an afterthought*) And is forgotten.

ESTRAGON (*moving to* L *of Vladimir*) In the meantime let's try and converse calmly, since we're incapable of keeping silent.

VLADIMIR. You're right, we're inexhaustible.

ESTRAGON (*moving to the barrel and sitting*) It's so we won't think.

VLADIMIR. We have that excuse.

ESTRAGON. It's so we won't hear.

VLADIMIR. We have our reasons.

ESTRAGON. All the dead voices.

VLADIMIR (*after a pause*) They make a noise like wings.

ESTRAGON. Like leaves.

VLADIMIR. Like sand.

ESTRAGON. Like leaves.

(*There is a silence*)

(lyrical beauty)

VLADIMIR. They all speak together.

ESTRAGON. Each one to itself.

(*There is a silence*)

crucifixtson
(sp?)

VLADIMIR. Rather they whisper.
ESTRAGON. They rustle.
VLADIMIR. They murmur.
ESTRAGON. They rustle.

people generally.

(*There is a silence*)

VLADIMIR. What do they say?
ESTRAGON. They talk about their lives.
VLADIMIR. To have lived is not enough for them.
ESTRAGON. They have to talk about it.
VLADIMIR. To be dead is not enough for them.
ESTRAGON. It is not sufficient.

(*There is a silence*)

VLADIMIR. They make a noise like feathers.
ESTRAGON. Like leaves.
VLADIMIR. Like ashes.
ESTRAGON. Like leaves.

(*There is a long silence*)

VLADIMIR. Say something.
ESTRAGON (*whispering*) I'm trying.

(*There is a long silence*)

language doesn't allow them to express themselves.

VLADIMIR (*in anguish*) Say anything at all.
ESTRAGON. What do we do now?
VLADIMIR. Wait for Godot.
ESTRAGON. Ah!

(*There is a silence*)

VLADIMIR. This is awful.
ESTRAGON. Sing something.
VLADIMIR. No, no. (*He ponders*) We could start all over again perhaps.
ESTRAGON. That should be easy.
VLADIMIR. It's the start that's difficult.
ESTRAGON. You can start from anything.
VLADIMIR. Yes, but you have to decide.
ESTRAGON (*deflated*) True.

can't make any decisions.

(*There is a long silence*)

VLADIMIR. Help me!
ESTRAGON. I'm trying.

(*There is a silence*)

VLADIMIR. When you seek you hear.
ESTRAGON. You do.
VLADIMIR. That prevents you from finding.

frustration of language.

Cannot communicate → non-sequitors
no indication of V & E common

ESTRAGON. It does.

VLADIMIR. That prevents you from thinking.

ESTRAGON. You think all the same.

VLADIMIR. No, no, it's impossible.

ESTRAGON. That's the idea, let's contradict each other.

VLADIMIR. Impossible.

ESTRAGON. You think so?

VLADIMIR. We're in no danger of ever thinking any more.

ESTRAGON. Then what are we complaining about?

VLADIMIR. Thinking is not the worst.

trying to avoid thinking.

ESTRAGON. Perhaps not. But at least there's that.

VLADIMIR. That what?

ESTRAGON. That's the idea, let's ask each other questions.

VLADIMIR. What do you mean, at least there's that?

ESTRAGON. That much less misery.

VLADIMIR. True.

ESTRAGON. Well? If we gave thanks for our mercies?

VLADIMIR. What is terrible is to have thought.

ESTRAGON. But did that ever happen to us?

VLADIMIR. Where are all these corpses from?

mind is where dead thoughts stored.

ESTRAGON. These skeletons.

VLADIMIR. Tell me that.

ESTRAGON. True.

VLADIMIR. We must have thought a little.

ESTRAGON. At the very beginning.

VLADIMIR. A charnel-house! A charnel-house!

bodies piled up.

ESTRAGON. You don't have to look.

VLADIMIR. You can't help looking.

ESTRAGON. True.

VLADIMIR. Try as one may.

ESTRAGON. I beg your pardon?

VLADIMIR. Try as one may.

ESTRAGON (*after a pause*) We should turn resolutely towards Nature.

VLADIMIR. We've tried that.

ESTRAGON. True.

VLADIMIR. Oh, it's not the worst, I know.

ESTRAGON. What?

VLADIMIR. To have thought.

ESTRAGON. Obviously.

VLADIMIR. But we could have done without it.

ESTRAGON. *Que voulez-vous?*

VLADIMIR. I beg your pardon?

what can you expect?

ESTRAGON. *Que voulez-vous?*

VLADIMIR. Ah! *Que voulez-vous.* Exactly.

(*There is a silence*)

ESTRAGON. That wasn't such a bad little canter.

...ting —1 as if not listening to othr.

VLADIMIR. Yes, but now we'll have to find something else.

ESTRAGON (*after a pause*) Let me see. (*He takes off his hat and concentrates*)

VLADIMIR. Let me see. (*He takes off his hat and concentrates*)

(*They concentrate*)

Ah!

(*They put on their hats and relax*)

ESTRAGON. Well?

VLADIMIR. What was I saying, we could go on from there.

ESTRAGON. What were you saying when?

VLADIMIR. At the very beginning.

ESTRAGON. The beginning of *what*?

VLADIMIR. This evening—I was saying—I was saying . . .

ESTRAGON (*turning away*) Don't ask me. I'm not a historian.

VLADIMIR (*rising and moving up* C) Wait—we embraced—we were happy—happy—what do we do now that we're happy—go on—waiting—waiting—let me think—it's coming—go on waiting —now that we're happy—let me see . . . Ah! (*He looks at the tree*) The tree!

ESTRAGON. The tree?

VLADIMIR. Do you not remember?

ESTRAGON. I'm tired.

VLADIMIR. Look at it.

(ESTRAGON *looks at the tree*)

ESTRAGON. I see nothing.

VLADIMIR. But yesterday evening it was all black and bare. And now it's covered with leaves.

ESTRAGON. Leaves?

VLADIMIR. In a single night.

ESTRAGON. It must be the spring.

VLADIMIR (*moving up* R) But in a single night.

ESTRAGON. I tell you we weren't *here* yesterday. Another of your nightmares.

VLADIMIR. And where were we yesterday evening according to you? (*He moves down* R *and crosses to* R *of Estragon*)

ESTRAGON. How do I know? In another compartment. There's no lack of void.

VLADIMIR (*sure of himself*) Good. We weren't here yesterday evening. Now what did we do yesterday evening? (*He sits on the mound*)

ESTRAGON. Do?

VLADIMIR. Try and remember.

ESTRAGON. Do? I suppose we blathered.

VLADIMIR (*controlling himself*) About what?

ESTRAGON. Oh—this and that, I suppose, nothing in particular. (*With assurance*) Yes, now I remember, yesterday evening we spent talking about nothing in particular. That's been going on now for half a century.

VLADIMIR. You don't remember any fact, any circumstance?

ESTRAGON (*wearily*) Don't torment me, Didi.

VLADIMIR. The sun. The moon. Do you not remember?

ESTRAGON. They must have been there, as usual.

VLADIMIR. You didn't notice anything out of the ordinary?

ESTRAGON. Alas!

VLADIMIR (*rising*) And Pozzo? And Lucky?

ESTRAGON. Pozzo?

VLADIMIR. The bones.

ESTRAGON. They were like fishbones.

VLADIMIR. It was Pozzo gave them to you.

ESTRAGON. I don't know.

VLADIMIR. And the kick?

ESTRAGON. That's right, someone gave me a kick.

VLADIMIR (*moving to* R *of the barrel*) It was Lucky gave it to you.

ESTRAGON. And all that was yesterday?

VLADIMIR. Show your leg.

ESTRAGON (*rising*) Which?

VLADIMIR. Both. Pull up your trousers.

(ESTRAGON *raises his left leg towards Vladimir, and staggers.* VLADIMIR *holds Estragon's leg. They stagger*)

Pull up your trousers.

ESTRAGON. I can't.

(VLADIMIR *pulls up the trouser leg, looks at the leg then releases it.* ESTRAGON *almost falls*)

VLADIMIR. The other.

(ESTRAGON *again lifts his left leg*)

The other, pig! (*He pushes Estragon*)

(ESTRAGON *loses his balance and almost falls*)

(*He catches Estragon's right leg from behind. Triumphantly*) There's the wound. Beginning to fester.

ESTRAGON. And what about it?

VLADIMIR (*releasing Estragon's leg*) Where are your boots?

ESTRAGON. I must have thrown them away.

VLADIMIR. When?

ESTRAGON. I don't know.

VLADIMIR. Why?

ESTRAGON (*exasperated*) I don't know why I don't know.

VLADIMIR. No, I mean, why did you throw them away?

ESTRAGON (*exasperated*) Because they were hurting me.

VLADIMIR (*pointing to the boots down* C; *triumphantly*) There they are.

(ESTRAGON *looks at the boots*)

At the very spot where you left them yesterday (*He pushes Estragon towards the boots*)

(ESTRAGON *closely inspects the boots, then moves* RC)

ESTRAGON. They're not mine.
VLADIMIR (*stupefied*) Not yours?
ESTRAGON. Mine were black. These are brown.
VLADIMIR. You're sure yours were black?
ESTRAGON. Well, they were a kind of grey.
VLADIMIR. And these are brown? Show.
ESTRAGON (*picking up a boot*) Well, they're a kind of green.
VLADIMIR (*moving to* L *of Estragon*) Show.

(ESTRAGON *thrusts the boot at* VLADIMIR, *who inspects it, and angrily throws it down*)

Well, of all the . . .
ESTRAGON. You see, all that's a lot of bloody . . .
VLADIMIR. Ah! I see what it is. Yes, I see what's happened.
ESTRAGON. All that's a lot of bloody . . .
VLADIMIR. It's elementary. Someone came and took yours and left you his.
ESTRAGON. Why?
VLADIMIR. His were too tight for him, so he took yours.
ESTRAGON. But mine were too tight.
VLADIMIR. For you. Not for him.
ESTRAGON (*moving* RC) I'm tired. (*He pauses*) Let's go.
VLADIMIR. We can't.
ESTRAGON. Why not?
VLADIMIR. We're waiting for Godot.
ESTRAGON. Ah (*He pauses. Despairingly*) What'll we do, what'll we do?
VLADIMIR. There's nothing we can do.
ESTRAGON. But I can't go on like this.
VLADIMIR (*moving to* L *of Estragon*) Would you like a radish?
ESTRAGON. Is that all there is?
VLADIMIR. There are radishes and turnips.
ESTRAGON. Are there no carrots?
VLADIMIR. No. Anyway, you overdo it with your carrots.
ESTRAGON. Then give me a radish.

(VLADIMIR *fumbles in his pockets, finds nothing but turnips, but finally brings out a radish and hands it to* ESTRAGON, *who examines it and sniffs it*)

It's black!
VLADIMIR. It's a radish.
ESTRAGON. I only like the pink ones, you know that.

VLADIMIR. Then you don't want it?
ESTRAGON. I only like the pink ones.
VLADIMIR. Then give it back to me.

(ESTRAGON *returns the radish to Vladimir*)

ESTRAGON. I'll go and get a carrot. (*He does not move*)
VLADIMIR. This is becoming really insignificant.
ESTRAGON. Not sufficiently.

yeah, no kidding.

(*There is a silence*)

VLADIMIR. What about trying them?
ESTRAGON. I've tried everything.
VLADIMIR. I mean the boots.
ESTRAGON (*after a pause*) Would that be a good thing?
VLADIMIR. It'd pass the time.

(ESTRAGON *hesitates*)

I assure you, it'd be an occupation.
ESTRAGON. A relaxation.
VLADIMIR. A recreation.
ESTRAGON. A relaxation.
VLADIMIR. Try.
ESTRAGON. You'll help me?
VLADIMIR. I will, of course. (*He moves* C *and kneels by the boots*)
ESTRAGON (*moving to* R *of Vladimir*) We don't manage too badly, eh, Didi, between the two of us?
VLADIMIR. Yes, yes. Come on, we'll try the left first.
ESTRAGON. We always find something, eh, Didi, to give us the impression that we exist?
VLADIMIR (*impatiently*) Yes, yes, we're magicians. But let us persevere in what we have resolved, before we forget. (*He picks up the left boot*) Come on, give me your foot.

(ESTRAGON *raises his right foot*)

The other, hog!

(ESTRAGON *raises his left foot over Vladimir's head*)

Higher!

(VLADIMIR *rises. Wreathed together they stagger about the stage*)

(*He succeeds finally in putting on the boot*) Try and walk.

(ESTRAGON *walks in a small circle*)

Well?
ESTRAGON. It fits.
VLADIMIR (*taking a piece of string from his pocket*) We'll try and lace it.
ESTRAGON (*vehemently*) No, no, no laces, no laces.
VLADIMIR. You'll be sorry. Let's try the other.

no ties.

(ESTRAGON *holds out his right foot.* VLADIMIR *puts on the boot, and they stagger about, as before*)

Try and walk.

(ESTRAGON *steps out of the boot and walks* R)

ESTRAGON. It fits, too.

(VLADIMIR *picks up the boot.* ESTRAGON *sits on the mound, puts on the boot, then rises and walks down* LC)

VLADIMIR. They don't hurt you?
ESTRAGON. Not yet.
VLADIMIR. Then you can keep them.
ESTRAGON. They're too big.
VLADIMIR. Perhaps you'll have socks some day.
ESTRAGON. True.
VLADIMIR. Then you'll keep them?
ESTRAGON. That's enough about these boots.
VLADIMIR. Yes, but . . .
ESTRAGON (*violently*) Enough! (*He pauses*) I suppose I might as well sit down. (*He looks around for a place to sit down, and sits on the mound*)
VLADIMIR (*crossing to* L *of Estragon*) That's where you were sitting yesterday evening.
ESTRAGON. If I could only sleep.
VLADIMIR (*sitting* L *of Estragon on the mound*) Yesterday you slept.
ESTRAGON. I'll try. (*He drops his head between his knees*)
VLADIMIR. Wait. (*He sings in a loud voice*)
                    Bye bye bye bye
                    Bye bye . . .
ESTRAGON (*looking up; angrily*) Not so loud.
VLADIMIR (*singing softly*)
                    Bye bye bye bye
                    Bye bye bye bye
                    Bye bye bye bye
                    Bye bye . . .

(ESTRAGON *sleeps.* VLADIMIR *rises softly, removes his coat, lays it across Estragon's shoulders, then paces up and down, swinging his arms to warm himself.* ESTRAGON *wakes with a start, rises and casts wildly about*)

(*He runs to Estragon and puts his arm around him*) There—there—I'm here—don't be afraid.
ESTRAGON. Ah!
VLADIMIR. There—there—it's all over.
ESTRAGON. I was falling . . .
VLADIMIR. It's all over, it's all over.
ESTRAGON. I was on top of a . . .
VLADIMIR. Don't tell me. Come, we'll walk it off.

[handwritten annotations: "2nd action." with arrow; "what happened in Act 1 as well."]

(VLADIMIR *takes* ESTRAGON *by the arm, walks him* L, *then leads him* R, *until* ESTRAGON *refuses to go any farther*)

ESTRAGON. That's enough. I'm tired.
VLADIMIR. You'd rather be stuck there doing nothing?
ESTRAGON. Yes.
VLADIMIR. Please yourself. (*He releases Estragon, picks up his coat and puts it on*)
ESTRAGON (*after a pause*) Let's go.
VLADIMIR. We can't.
ESTRAGON. Why not?
VLADIMIR. We're waiting for Godot.
ESTRAGON. Ah! (*He moves to the mound and sits*)

(VLADIMIR *paces down* L, *then turns and paces down* R)

Can you not stay still?
VLADIMIR. I'm cold.
ESTRAGON. We came too early.
VLADIMIR. It's always at nightfall.
ESTRAGON. But night doesn't fall.
VLADIMIR. It'll fall all of a sudden, like yesterday.
ESTRAGON. Then it'll be night?
VLADIMIR. And we can go.
ESTRAGON. Then it'll be day again. (*He pauses. Despairingly*) What'll we do, what'll we do?
VLADIMIR (*crossing to* LC; *violently*) Will you stop whining! I've had about my belly full of your lamentations.
ESTRAGON. I'm going.
VLADIMIR (*seeing Lucky's hat*) Well!
ESTRAGON. Good-bye.
VLADIMIR. Lucky's hat. (*He moves to the hat*) I've been here an hour and never saw it. (*Very pleased*) Fine!
ESTRAGON. You'll never see me again.
VLADIMIR. I knew it was the right place. Now our troubles are over. (*He picks up the hat, contemplates it and straightens it*) Must have been a very handsome hat. (*He moves to* R *of Estragon, removes his own hat and puts Lucky's hat on his head. He hands his own hat to Estragon*) Here.
ESTRAGON What?
VLADIMIR. Hold that.

(ESTRAGON *takes Vladimir's hat.* VLADIMIR *adjusts Lucky's hat on his head.* ESTRAGON *puts on Vladimir's hat in place of his own which he hands to Vladimir.* VLADIMIR *takes Estragon's hat.* ESTRAGON *adjusts Vladimir's hat on his head.* VLADIMIR *puts on Estragon's hat in place of Lucky's, which he hands to Estragon.* ESTRAGON *takes Lucky's hat.* VLADIMIR *adjusts Estragon's hat on his head.* ESTRAGON *puts on Lucky's hat in place of Vladimir's which he hands to Vladimir.* VLADIMIR *takes his hat.* ESTRAGON *adjusts Lucky's hat on his head.*

VLADIMIR *puts on his hat in place of Estragon's which he hands to Estragon.* ESTRAGON *takes his hat.* VLADIMIR *adjusts his hat on his head.* ESTRAGON *puts on his hat in place of Lucky's which he hands to Vladimir.* VLADIMIR *takes Lucky's hat.* ESTRAGON *adjusts his hat on his head.* VLADIMIR *puts on Lucky's hat in place of his own which he hands to Estragon.* ESTRAGON *takes Vladimir's hat.* VLADIMIR *adjusts Lucky's hat on his head.* ESTRAGON *hands Vladimir's hat back to* VLADIMIR, *who takes it and hands it back to* ESTRAGON *who takes it and hands it back to* VLADIMIR, *who takes it and throws it down*)

How does it fit me?

ESTRAGON. How would I know?

VLADIMIR. No, but how do I look in it? (*He turns his head coquettishly to and fro and minces down* RC, *like a mannequin*)

ESTRAGON. Hideous.

VLADIMIR. But not more so than usual?

ESTRAGON. Neither more nor less.

VLADIMIR. Then I can keep it. Mine irked me. (*He pauses*) How shall I say? (*He pauses*) It itched me. (*He takes off Lucky's hat, peers into it, shakes it, knocks on the crown, then replaces it on his head*)

ESTRAGON. I'm going.

(*There is a silence*)

VLADIMIR. Will you not play?

ESTRAGON. Play at what?

VLADIMIR. We could play at Pozzo and Lucky.

ESTRAGON. Never heard of it.

VLADIMIR. I'll do Lucky, you do Pozzo. (*He imitates the attitude of Lucky staggering under the weight of his baggage, and crosses down* L)

(ESTRAGON *looks at him with stupefaction*)

Go on!

ESTRAGON. What am I to do?

VLADIMIR. Curse me!

ESTRAGON (*after reflecting*) Naughty!

VLADIMIR. Stronger.

ESTRAGON. Gonococcus! Civil Servant!

[handwritten note: Beckett hated civil servants.]

(VLADIMIR *sways back and forth, doubled in two*)

VLADIMIR. Tell me to think.

ESTRAGON. What?

VLADIMIR. Say, "Think, pig!"

ESTRAGON. Think, pig!

(*There is a pause.* VLADIMIR *squeaks*)

That's enough of that.

VLADIMIR. Tell me to dance.

ESTRAGON. I'm going.

VLADIMIR. Dance, hog! (*He writhes where he stands*)

(ESTRAGON *rises and exits precipitately* R)

I can't. (*He looks up and misses Estragon*) Gogo! (*He moves wildly about the stage*)

(ESTRAGON, *panting, enters* R, *sees Vladimir, and turns to go*)

(*He moves to Estragon*) There you are again at last.

(*They grasp each other*)

ESTRAGON (*panting*) I'm accursed!
VLADIMIR. Where were you? I thought you were gone for ever.
ESTRAGON. They're coming.
VLADIMIR. Who?
ESTRAGON. I don't know.
VLADIMIR. How many?
ESTRAGON. I don't know.
VLADIMIR (*triumphantly*) It's Godot! At last. Gogo! It's Godot.
We're saved! Let's go and meet him. (*He drags Estragon* R)

Estragon is Panicky.

(ESTRAGON *resists, pulls himself free, crosses and exits* L)

Gogo! Come back! (*He turns and scans the horizon off* R)

(ESTRAGON *enters backwards* L, *crosses and falls into Vladimir's arms*)

There you are again, again.
ESTRAGON. I'm in hell.
VLADIMIR. Where were you?
ESTRAGON. They're coming there, too. —   *who is 'they'?*
VLADIMIR. We're surrounded!

(ESTRAGON *rushes wildly up* C)

Imbecile! (*He follows Estragon*) There's no way out there. (*He takes Estragon by the arm, drags him down* C *and gestures towards the auditorium*) There! Not a soul in sight! Off you go. Quick! (*He pushes Estragon towards the auditorium*)

(ESTRAGON *recoils in horror*)

You won't? (*He contemplates the auditorium*) Well, I can understand that. Wait till I see. (*He reflects*) Your only hope left is to disappear.
ESTRAGON. Where?
VLADIMIR. Behind the tree.

(ESTRAGON *hesitates*)

Quick! Behind the tree.

(ESTRAGON *goes and crouches behind the tree*)

(He moves behind Estragon, pushes his back out of sight, then moves and pushes his head out of sight) Decidedly this tree will not have been of the slightest use to us.

ESTRAGON *(emerging from the tree; calmer)* I lost my head. *(He bows his head for shame)* Forgive me. *(He raises his head with spirit)* It won't happen again. Tell me what to do.

VLADIMIR. There's nothing to do.

ESTRAGON *(leading Vladimir down L)* You go and stand there. *(He places him facing L)* There, don't move and watch out.

(VLADIMIR scans the horizon off L, shading his eyes with his hand)

(He runs to R, stands with his back to Vladimir, and scans the horizon off R, shading his eyes with his hand) Back to back like in the good old days.

(They turn their heads, look at each other for a moment, then resume their watch. There is a long silence)

Do you not see anything coming?

VLADIMIR *(turning his head)* What?

ESTRAGON *(louder)* Do you not see anything coming?

VLADIMIR. No.

ESTRAGON. Neither do I.

(They resume their watch. There is a long silence)

VLADIMIR. You must have had a vision.

ESTRAGON *(turning his head)* What?

VLADIMIR *(louder)* You must have had a vision.

ESTRAGON. No need to shout.

(They resume their watch. There is a long silence, then they turn simultaneously)

VLADIMIR ⎫
ESTRAGON ⎬ *(together)* Do you . . . ?

VLADIMIR. Oh, pardon!

ESTRAGON. Carry on.

VLADIMIR. No, no, after you.

ESTRAGON. No, no, you first.

VLADIMIR. I interrupted you.

ESTRAGON. On the contrary.

(They glare angrily at each other)

VLADIMIR. Ceremonious ape!

ESTRAGON. Punctilious pig!

VLADIMIR *(violently)* Finish your phrase, I tell you.

ESTRAGON. Finish your own.

(There is a silence, during which ESTRAGON moves a step or two RC, and VLADIMIR a step or two LC)

VLADIMIR. Moron!
ESTRAGON. That's the idea, let's abuse each other.

(*They turn, increase the space between them, turn again and face each other*)

VLADIMIR. Moron!
ESTRAGON. Vermin!
VLADIMIR. Abortion!
ESTRAGON. Morpion!
VLADIMIR. Sewer-rat!
ESTRAGON. Curate!
VLADIMIR. Cretin!
ESTRAGON (*with finality*) Crritic!
VLADIMIR. Oh! (*He wilts, vanquished, and turns away*)
ESTRAGON. Now let's make it up.

(*They move and meet c*)

VLADIMIR. Gogo!
ESTRAGON. Didi!
VLADIMIR. Your hand!
ESTRAGON. Take it!
VLADIMIR. Come to my arms.
ESTRAGON. Your arms?
VLADIMIR. My breast.
ESTRAGON. Off we go.

(*They embrace, then separate*)

VLADIMIR (*after a pause*) How time flies when one has fun.
ESTRAGON (*after a pause*) What do we do now?
VLADIMIR. While waiting?
ESTRAGON. While waiting.
VLADIMIR (*after a pause*) We could do our exercises.
ESTRAGON. Our movements.
VLADIMIR. Our elevations.
ESTRAGON. Our relaxations.
VLADIMIR. Our elongations.
ESTRAGON. Our relaxations.
VLADIMIR. To warm us up.
ESTRAGON. To calm us down.
VLADIMIR. Off we go. (*He hops from one foot to the other*)

(ESTRAGON *imitates Vladimir*)

ESTRAGON (*stopping*) That's enough. I'm tired.
VLADIMIR (*stopping*) We're not in form. What about a little deep breathing?
ESTRAGON. I'm tired breathing.
VLADIMIR. You're right. (*He pauses*) Let's just do the tree, for our balance.

ESTRAGON. The tree?

(VLADIMIR *does the tree, staggering about on one leg*)

VLADIMIR (*stopping*) Your turn.

(ESTRAGON *does the tree, staggering about on one leg*)

ESTRAGON. Do you think God sees me?
VLADIMIR. You must close your eyes.

(ESTRAGON *closes his eyes and staggers down* R)

ESTRAGON (*brandishing his fists; at the top of his voice*) God have
pity on me.
VLADIMIR (*moving to* L *of Estragon; vexed*) And me.
ESTRAGON (*brandishing his fists; at the top of his voice*) On me! On
me! Pity! On me!

(POZZO *and* LUCKY *enter* L. POZZO *is now blind*. LUCKY *is
burdened as before.* POZZO *drives him with the rope, but it is much
shorter so that* POZZO *may follow more easily.* LUCKY *wears a different
hat.* ESTRAGON *sees Pozzo.* VLADIMIR *turns and looks* L. LUCKY *and*
POZZO *cross and go up* R. LUCKY *stops suddenly and* POZZO, *continuing on his way, bumps into him*)

VLADIMIR. Gogo! (*He crosses to* C)

(ESTRAGON *crosses to* L *of Vladimir.* LUCKY *totters*)

POZZO (*clutching Lucky*) What is it? Who is it?

(LUCKY *falls to the ground, drops everything and brings* POZZO
down with him. *They remain stretched out motionless among the scattered
baggage*)

ESTRAGON. Is it Godot?
VLADIMIR. At last! Reinforcements at last.
POZZO. Help!
ESTRAGON. Is it Godot?
VLADIMIR. We were beginning to weaken. Now we're sure to
see the evening out.
POZZO. Help!
ESTRAGON. Do you hear him?
VLADIMIR. We're no longer alone, waiting for the night, wait-
ing for Godot, waiting for—waiting. All evening we have strug-
gled, unassisted. Now it's over. It's already tomorrow.
POZZO. Help!
VLADIMIR. Time flows again already. The sun will set, the
moon will rise, and we'll away—from here.
POZZO. Pity!
VLADIMIR. Poor Pozzo.
ESTRAGON. I knew it was him.

VLADIMIR. Who?
ESTRAGON. Godot.
VLADIMIR. But it's not Godot.
ESTRAGON (*after a pause*) It's not Godot?
VLADIMIR. It's not Godot.
ESTRAGON (*after a pause*) Then who is it?
VLADIMIR. It's Pozzo.
POZZO. Here! Here! Help me up.
VLADIMIR. He can't get up.
ESTRAGON. Let's go.
VLADIMIR. We can't.
ESTRAGON. Why not?
VLADIMIR. We're waiting for Godot.
ESTRAGON. Ah! (*He turns to go, but stops when Vladimir speaks*)
VLADIMIR. Perhaps he has another bone for you.
ESTRAGON. Bone?
VLADIMIR. Chicken. Do you not remember?
ESTRAGON. It was him?
VLADIMIR. Yes.
ESTRAGON. Ask him.
VLADIMIR. Perhaps we should help him first.
ESTRAGON. To do what?
VLADIMIR. To get up.
ESTRAGON. He can't get up?
VLADIMIR. He wants to get up.
ESTRAGON. Then let him get up.
VLADIMIR. He can't.
ESTRAGON. Why not?
VLADIMIR. I don't know.

(POZZO *writhes, groans and beats the ground with his fists*)

ESTRAGON. We should ask him for the bone first. Then if he refuses we'll leave him there.
VLADIMIR. You mean we have him at our mercy?
ESTRAGON. Yes.
VLADIMIR. And that we should subordinate our good offices to certain conditions?
ESTRAGON. Yes.
VLADIMIR. That seems intelligent all right. But there's one thing I'm afraid of.
POZZO. Help!
ESTRAGON. What?
VLADIMIR. That Lucky might get going all of a sudden. Then we'd be banjoed.
ESTRAGON. Lucky?
VLADIMIR. He's the one went for you yesterday.
ESTRAGON. I tell you there was ten of them.
VLADIMIR. No, before that, the one that kicked you.

ESTRAGON. Is he there?

VLADIMIR. As large as life. (*He gestures towards Lucky*) For the moment he is inert. But he might run amuck any minute.

POZZO. Help!

ESTRAGON. And suppose we gave him a good beating: the two of us?

VLADIMIR. You mean if we fell on him in his sleep?

ESTRAGON. Yes.

VLADIMIR. That seems a good idea all right. But could we do it? Is he really asleep? (*He pauses*) No, the best would be to take advantage of Pozzo's calling for help.

POZZO. Help!

VLADIMIR. To help him . . .

ESTRAGON. *We* help *him*?

VLADIMIR. In anticipation of some tangible return.

ESTRAGON. And suppose he . . ?

VLADIMIR. Let us not waste our time in idle discourse. (*He pauses then moves and stands on the mound. Vehemently*) Let us rather do something, while we have the chance. It is not every day that we are needed. Not indeed that *we personally* are needed. *Others* would meet the case equally well, if not better. To all mankind they were addressed, those cries for help still ringing in our ears. But, at this place, at this moment of time, all mankind is us, whether we like it or not. Let us make the most of it, before it is too late. Let us represent worthily for once, the foul brood to which a cruel fate has consigned us. What do you say?

(ESTRAGON *says nothing*)

It is true, that when with folded arms we weigh the pros and cons, we are no less a credit to our species. The tiger bounds to the help of his congeners without the least reflection or else he slinks away into the depths of the thickets. But that is not the question. What are we doing here, *that* is the question. And we are blessed in this, that we happen to know the answer. Yes, in this immense confusion one thing alone is clear. We are waiting for Godot to come——

ESTRAGON. Ah!

POZZO. Help!

VLADIMIR. —or for night to fall. (*He pauses*) We have kept our appointment, and that's an end to that. We are not saints, but we have kept our appointment. How many people can boast as much?

ESTRAGON. Billions.

VLADIMIR. You think so?

ESTRAGON. I don't know.

VLADIMIR. You may be right.

POZZO. Help!

VLADIMIR. What's certain is that the hours are long under

these conditions, and constrain us to beguile them with proceedings which, how shall I say, which may at first sight seem reasonable until they become a habit. You may say it is to prevent our reason from foundering. No doubt. But has it not long been straying in the night without end of the abyssal depths? That's what I sometimes wonder. You follow my reasoning?

ESTRAGON (*aphoristically*) We all are born mad. Some remain so.

POZZO. Help! I'll pay you.

ESTRAGON. How much?

POZZO. Two shillings.

ESTRAGON. Not enough.

echo of Shakespeare.

VLADIMIR. I wouldn't go so far as that.

ESTRAGON. You think it's enough?

VLADIMIR. No, I mean so far as to assert that I was weak in the head when I came into the world. But that is not the question.

POZZO. Five shillings.

VLADIMIR. We wait. (*He gets off the mound*) We are bored. (*He throws up his hand*) No, don't protest, we are bored to death, there's no denying it. Good. A diversion comes along and what do we do? We let it go to waste. Come, let's get to work. (*He crosses to R of Pozzo*) In an instant all will vanish and we'll be alone again, in the midst of nothingness. (*He broods*)

POZZO. Five shillings.

VLADIMIR. We're coming. (*He tries to pull Pozzo to his feet, fails, tries again, stumbles, falls, tries to get up, but fails*)

(POZZO *sits up*)

ESTRAGON. What's the matter with you all?

VLADIMIR. Help!

ESTRAGON. I'm going.

VLADIMIR. Don't leave me. They'll kill me.

POZZO. Where am I?

VLADIMIR. Gogo!

POZZO. Help!

VLADIMIR. Help!

ESTRAGON. I'm going.

VLADIMIR. Help me up first. Then we'll go together.

ESTRAGON. You promise?

VLADIMIR. I swear it.

ESTRAGON. And we'll never come back?

VLADIMIR. Never.

ESTRAGON (*moving to L of Pozzo*) We'll go to the Pyrenees.

VLADIMIR. Wherever you like.

POZZO. Ten shillings. A pound.

ESTRAGON. I've always wanted to wander in the Pyrenees.

VLADIMIR. You'll wander in them.

ESTRAGON (*recoiling*) Who belched? (*He moves* LC)

VLADIMIR. Pozzo.
Pozzo. Here! Here! Pity!
ESTRAGON. It's revolting.
VLADIMIR. Quick! Give me your hand.
ESTRAGON. I'm going. (*He pauses. Louder*) I'm going.
VLADIMIR. Well, I suppose in the end I'll get up under my own steam. (*He attempts to rise, but fails*) In the fullness of time.
ESTRAGON. What's the matter with you?
VLADIMIR. Go to hell.
ESTRAGON. Are you staying there?
VLADIMIR. For the time being.
ESTRAGON (*moving to Vladimir*) Come on, get up, you'll catch a chill.
VLADIMIR. Don't worry about me.
ESTRAGON. Come on, Didi, don't be pig-headed (*He stretches out his hand to Vladimir*)
VLADIMIR (*hastily seizing Estragon's hand*) Pull!

(ESTRAGON *pulls, stumbles and falls* L *of Pozzo*)

Pozzo. Help.
VLADIMIR. We've arrived.
Pozzo. Who are you?
VLADIMIR. We are men.
ESTRAGON (*after a pause*) Sweet mother earth.
VLADIMIR. Can you get up?
ESTRAGON. I don't know.
VLADIMIR. Try.
ESTRAGON. Not now, not now.

(*There is a silence*)

Pozzo. What's happened?
VLADIMIR (*violently*) Will you stop it, you! Pest! He thinks of nothing but himself.
ESTRAGON. What about a little snooze?
VLADIMIR. Did you hear him? He wants to know what happened.
ESTRAGON, Don't mind him. Sleep. (*He falls asleep*)

(*There is a silence*)

Pozzo. Pity! Pity!
ESTRAGON (*with a start*) What is it?
VLADIMIR. Were you asleep?
ESTRAGON. I must have been.
VLADIMIR. It's this bastard Pozzo at it again.
ESTRAGON. Tell him to stop it. Kick him in the crotch.
VLADIMIR (*striking Pozzo*) Will you stop it! Crablouse!

(Pozzo, *with cries of pain, extricates himself and crawls away* L. *Now and then he stops, blindly saws the air, and calls for help*)

(*He props himself on his elbow and observes Pozzo's retreat*) He's off.

  (POZZO *collapses by the barrel*)

He's down.

ESTRAGON. What do we do now?

VLADIMIR. Perhaps I could crawl to him.

ESTRAGON. Don't leave me.

VLADIMIR. Or I could call to him.

ESTRAGON. Yes, call to him.

VLADIMIR (*calling*) Pozzo! (*He pauses*) Pozzo! (*He pauses*) No
reply.

ESTRAGON. Together.

VLADIMIR ⎫
ESTRAGON ⎬ (*together; calling*) Pozzo! Pozzo!

VLADIMIR. He moved.

ESTRAGON. Are you sure his name is Pozzo?

VLADIMIR (*alarmed*) Mr Pozzo! Come back. We won't touch
you.

  (*There is a silence*)

ESTRAGON. We might try him with other names.

VLADIMIR. I'm afraid he's dying.

ESTRAGON. It'd be amusing.

VLADIMIR. What'd be amusing?

ESTRAGON. To try him with other names, one after the other.
That'd pass the time And we'd be bound to hit on the right one
sooner or later.

VLADIMIR. I tell you his name is Pozzo.

ESTRAGON. We'll soon see. (*He reflects*) Abel! Abel!

POZZO. Help!

VLADIMIR. Got it in one.

VLADIMIR. I begin to weary of this motif.

ESTRAGON. Perhaps the other is called Cain. (*He calls*) Cain!
Cain!

POZZO. Help!

ESTRAGON. He's all mankind. (*He pauses*) Look at the little
cloud.

VLADIMIR (*raising his eyes*) Where?

ESTRAGON. There. In the zenith.

VLADIMIR. Well? (*He pauses*) What is there so wonderful about
it?

  (*There is a silence*)

ESTRAGON. Let's pass on now to something else, do you mind?

VLADIMIR. I was just going to suggest it.

ESTRAGON. But to what?

VLADIMIR. Ah!

  (*There is a silence*)

ESTRAGON. Suppose we got up to begin with?
VLADIMIR. No harm trying.

(*They get up, by sitting back to back and pushing*)

ESTRAGON. Child's play.
VLADIMIR. Simple question of will-power.
ESTRAGON. And now?
POZZO. Help!
ESTRAGON. Let's go.
VLADIMIR. We can't.
ESTRAGON. Why not?
VLADIMIR. We're waiting for Godot.
ESTRAGON. Ah! (*He pauses. Despairingly*) What'll we do, what'll we do?
POZZO. Help!
VLADIMIR. What about helping him?
ESTRAGON. What does he want?
VLADIMIR. He wants to get up.
ESTRAGON. Then why doesn't he?
VLADIMIR. He wants us to help him to get up.
ESTRAGON. Then why don't we? What are we waiting for?

(VLADIMIR *and* ESTRAGON *move to* POZZO, *help him to his feet, then release him.* POZZO *immediately falls to the ground down* L)

VLADIMIR. We must hold him.

(*They raise* POZZO *to his feet. He sags between them, his arms round their necks*)

He must get used to being erect again. (*To Pozzo*) Feeling better?
POZZO. Who are you?
VLADIMIR. Do you not recognize us?
POZZO. I am blind.

(*There is a silence*)

ESTRAGON. Perhaps he can see into the future.
VLADIMIR (*to Pozzo*) Since when?
POZZO. I used to have wonderful sight—but are you friends?
ESTRAGON (*laughing noisily*) He wants to know if we are friends.
VLADIMIR. No, he means friends of his.
ESTRAGON. Well?
VLADIMIR. We've proved we are, by helping him.
ESTRAGON. Exactly. Would we have helped him if we weren't his friends?
VLADIMIR. Possibly.
ESTRAGON. True.
VLADIMIR. Don't let's quibble about that now.
POZZO. You are not highwaymen?
ESTRAGON. Highwaymen! Do we look like highwaymen?

Good Samaritan reference.

VLADIMIR. Damn it, can't you see the man is blind!
ESTRAGON. Damn it, so he is. (*He pauses*) Or so he says.
POZZO. Don't leave me.
VLADIMIR. No question of it.
ESTRAGON. For the moment.
POZZO. What time is it?   *theme of play.*
VLADIMIR (*inspecting the sky*) Seven o'clock—eight o'clock . . .
ESTRAGON. That depends what time of year it is.
POZZO. Is it evening?

(*There is a silence, during which* VLADIMIR *and* ESTRAGON *scrutinize the sunset*)

ESTRAGON. It looks as if it was rising backwards.
VLADIMIR. Impossible.
ESTRAGON. Perhaps it's the dawn.
VLADIMIR. Don't be a fool. It's the west over there.
ESTRAGON. How do you know?
POZZO (*anguished*) Is it evening?
VLADIMIR. Anyway, it hasn't moved.
ESTRAGON. I tell you it's rising.
POZZO. Why don't you answer?
ESTRAGON. Give us a chance.
VLADIMIR (*reassuringly*) It's evening, sir, it's evening, nigth is drawing nigh. My friend here would have me doubt it and I must confess he shook me for a moment. But it is not for nothing that I have lived through this long day and I can assure you it is very near the end of its repertory. (*He pauses*) How do you feel now?
ESTRAGON. How much longer must we cart him round?

(*They half release* POZZO, *but catch him again as he falls*)

We are not caryatides.
VLADIMIR. You were saying that your sight used to be good, if I heard you right.
POZZO. Wonderful! Wonderful, wonderfu! sight.

(*There is a silence*)

ESTRAGON (*irritably*) Expand! Expand!
VLADIMIR. Let him alone. Can't you see he's thinking of the days when he was happy? (*He pauses*) *Memoria praeteritorum bonorum*—that must be unpleasant.   *memory of past happiness.*
ESTRAGON. We wouldn't know.
VLADIMIR (*to Pozzo*) And it came on you all of a sudden?
POZZO. Quite wonderful!
VLADIMIR. I'm asking you if it came on you all of a sudden?
POZZO. I woke up one fine day as blind as Fortune. (*He pauses*) Sometimes I wonder if I'm not still asleep.
VLADIMIR. When was that?

POZZO. I don't know.

VLADIMIR. But no later than yesterday . . .

POZZO. Don't question me. The blind have no notion of time. The things of time are hidden from them, too.

VLADIMIR. Well, just fancy that. I could have sworn it was the opposite.

ESTRAGON. I'm going.

POZZO. Where are we?

VLADIMIR. I couldn't tell you.

POZZO. It isn't by any chance the place known as the Board?

VLADIMIR. Never heard of it.

POZZO. What is it like?

VLADIMIR (*looking around*) You couldn't describe it. It's like nothing. There's nothing. There's a tree.

POZZO. Then it's not the Board.

ESTRAGON (*sagging*) Some diversion!

POZZO. Where is my menial?

VLADIMIR. He's about somewhere.

POZZO. Why doesn't he answer when I call?

VLADIMIR. I don't know. He seems to be sleeping. Perhaps he's dead

POZZO. What happened exactly?

ESTRAGON. Exactly!

VLADIMIR. The two of you slipped. (*He pauses*) And fell.

POZZO. Go and see is he hurt.

VLADIMIR. But we can't leave you.

POZZO. You needn't both go.

VLADIMIR (*to Estragon*) You go.

ESTRAGON. After what he did to me? Never!

POZZO. Yes, yes, let your friend go, he stinks so. (*He pauses*) What is he waiting for?

VLADIMIR. What are you waiting for?

ESTRAGON. I'm waiting for Godot.

VLADIMIR (*after a pause*) What exactly should he do?

POZZO. Well, to begin with he should pull on the rope, as hard as he likes so long as he doesn't strangle him. He usually responds to that. If not he should give him a taste of his boot, in the face and the guts as far as possible.

VLADIMIR (*to Estragon*) You see, you've nothing to be afraid of. It's even an opportunity to revenge yourself.

ESTRAGON. And if he defends himself?

POZZO. No, no, he never defends himself.

VLADIMIR. I'll come flying to the rescue.

ESTRAGON. Don't take your eyes off me. (*He crosses to Lucky and stands above him*)

VLADIMIR. Make sure he's alive before you start. No point in exerting yourself if he's dead.

ESTRAGON (*bending over Lucky*) He's breathing.

VLADIMIR. Then let him have it.

(ESTRAGON, *with sudden fury, kicks Lucky, hurling abuse at him as he does so.* LUCKY *rolls down* RC. ESTRAGON *hurts his foot and limps to the mound*)

ESTRAGON. Oh, the brute! (*He sits on the mound, tries to take off his boots, but soon desists and disposes himself for sleep, his arms on his knees and his head on his arms*)

POZZO. What's gone wrong now?

VLADIMIR. My friend has hurt himself.

POZZO. And Lucky?

VLADIMIR. So it is he?

POZZO. What?

VLADIMIR. It is Lucky?

POZZO. I don't understand.

VLADIMIR. And you are Pozzo?

POZZO. Certainly I am Pozzo.

VLADIMIR. The same as yesterday?

POZZO. Yesterday?

VLADIMIR. We met yesterday. (*He pauses*) Do you not remember?

POZZO. I don't remember having met anyone yesterday. But tomorrow I won't remember having met anyone today. So don't count on me to enlighten you.

VLADIMIR. But . . .

POZZO. That's enough. (*He calls to Lucky*) Up, pig!

VLADIMIR. You were bringing him to the fair to sell him. You spoke to us. He danced. He thought. You had your sight.

POZZO. As you please. Let me go.

(VLADIMIR *moves aside*)

(*He moves towards Lucky*) Up!

(LUCKY *rises, moves up* RC *and gathers up his burdens*)

VLADIMIR. Where do you go from here?

POZZO (*following Lucky up* RC) I don't concern myself with that.

(LUCKY, *laden down, takes his place before Pozzo*)

Whip!

(LUCKY *puts everything down, looks for the whip, finds it, puts it into Pozzo's hand, then takes up everything again*)

Rope!

(LUCKY *puts everything down, puts the end of the rope into Pozzo's hand, then takes up everything again*)

VLADIMIR. What is there in the bag?

POZZO. Sand. (*He jerks the rope*) March!

VLADIMIR. Don't go yet.

POZZO. I'm going.

VLADIMIR. What do you do when you fall far from help?

POZZO. We wait till we can get up. Then we go on. (*To Lucky*) On!

VLADIMIR (*crossing to Pozzo*) Before you go, tell him to sing.

POZZO. Who?

VLADIMIR. Lucky.

POZZO. To sing?

VLADIMIR. Yes. Or to think. Or to recite.

POZZO. But he's dumb.

VLADIMIR (*after a pause*) Dumb!

POZZO. Dumb. He can't even groan.

VLADIMIR. Dumb! Since when?

POZZO (*suddenly furious*) Have you not done tormenting me with your accursed time? It's abominable. When! When! One day, is that not enough for you, one day like any other day, one day he went dumb, one day I went blind, one day we'll go deaf, one day we were born, one day we'll die, the same day, the same second, is that not enough for you? (*Calmer*) They give birth astride of a grave, the light gleams an instant, then it's night once more. (*He jerks the rope*) On!

(LUCKY *and* POZZO *exit up* R. VLADIMIR *looks after them. The noise of a fall off, reinforced by* VLADIMIR's *mimicry, announces that Lucky and Pozzo have fallen. There is a silence, during which* VLADIMIR *crosses to* L *of Estragon and contemplates him. After a few moments* VLADIMIR *shakes* ESTRAGON *who wakes with wild gesture and incoherent words*)

ESTRAGON (*finally*) Why will you never let me sleep?

VLADIMIR. I felt lonely.

ESTRAGON. I was dreaming I was happy.

VLADIMIR. That passed the time.

ESTRAGON. I was dreaming that . .

VLADIMIR. Don't tell me. (*He pauses, moves to the barrel and sits*) I wonder is he really blind?

ESTRAGON. Blind? Who?

VLADIMIR. Pozzo.

ESTRAGON. Blind?

VLADIMIR. He told us he was blind.

ESTRAGON. Well, what about it?

VLADIMIR. It seemed to me he saw us.

ESTRAGON. You dreamt it. (*He pauses*) Let's go. We can't. Ah! (*He pauses*) Are you sure it wasn't him?

VLADIMIR. Who?

ESTRAGON. Godot.

VLADIMIR. But who?

ESTRAGON. Pozzo.

VLADIMIR. Not at all. Not at all. (*He pauses*) Not at all.

ESTRAGON. I suppose I might as well get up. (*He rises painfully*) Ow! Didi!

VLADIMIR. I don't know what to think any more.

ESTRAGON. My feet! (*He sits on the mound and tries to take off his boots*) Help me!

VLADIMIR. Was I sleeping, while the others suffered? Am I sleeping now? Tomorrow, when I wake, or think I do, what shall I say of today? That with Estragon, my friend, at this place, until the fall of night, I waited for Godot? That Pozzo passed, with his carrier, and talked to us? Probably. But in all that what truth will there be?

(ESTRAGON, *having struggled in vain with his boots, dozes*)

(*He looks at Estragon*) He'll know nothing. He'll tell me about the blows he received and I'll give him a carrot. (*He pauses*) Astride of a grave, and a difficult birth. Down in the hole, lingeringly, the grave-digger puts on the forceps. We have time to grow old. The air is full of our cries. (*He listens*) But habit is a great deadener. (*He looks at Estragon*) At me, too, someone is looking, of me, too, someone is saying, "He is sleeping, he knows nothing, let him sleep on". (*He pauses*) I can't go on. (*He pauses*) What have I said? (*He broods*)

(*The* BOY *enters up* R *and crosses to* LC)

BOY. Please, Mister . . .

(VLADIMIR *turns and looks at the Boy*)

Mr Albert?

VLADIMIR. Off we go again. (*He pauses*) Do you not recognize me?

BOY. No, sir.

VLADIMIR. It wasn't you came yesterday?

BOY. No, sir.

VLADIMIR. This is your first time?

BOY. Yes, sir.

VLADIMIR (*after a pause*) You have a message from Mr Godot.

BOY. Yes, sir.

VLADIMIR. He won't come this evening.

BOY. No, sir.

VLADIMIR. But he'll come tomorrow.

BOY. Yes, sir.

VLADIMIR. Without fail.

BOY. Yes, sir.

(*There is a silence*)

VLADIMIR. Did you meet anyone?

BOY. No, sir.

VLADIMIR. Two other—(*he hesitates*) men?
BOY. I didn't see anyone, sir.
VLADIMIR (*after a pause*) What does he do, Mr Godot?

   (*The* BOY *is silent*)

Do you hear me?
BOY. Yes, sir.
VLADIMIR. Well?
BOY. He does nothing, sir.
VLADIMIR (*after a pause*) How is your brother?
BOY. He's sick, sir.
VLADIMIR. Perhaps it was he came yesterday?
BOY. I don't know, sir.
VLADIMIR (*after a pause; softly*) Has he a beard, Mr Godot?
BOY. Yes, sir.
VLADIMIR. Dark or—(*he hesitates*) or fair?
BOY. I think it's white, sir.
VLADIMIR (*after a pause*) Christ have mercy on us!
BOY (*after a pause*) What am I to say to Mr Godot, sir?
VLADIMIR. Tell him—(*he hesitates*) tell him you saw me and
that—(*he hesitates*) that you saw me. (*He pauses, rises and advances
on the Boy*)

   (*The* BOY *recoils*)

(*He halts*) You're sure you saw me, eh? You won't come and tell
me tomorrow that you never saw me before?

   (*There is a silence, then* VLADIMIR *makes a sudden spring forward.
The* BOY *avoids Vladimir and runs off up* R. *There is a silence.
The sun sets, the moon rises as before.* VLADIMIR *stands motionless and
bowed.* ESTRAGON *wakes, takes off his boots, rises with them in his
hands, moves and puts the boots on the ground down* C. *He then turns
and looks at Vladimir*)

ESTRAGON. What's wrong with you?
VLADIMIR. Nothing.
ESTRAGON. I'm going.
VLADIMIR. So am I.
ESTRAGON. Was I long asleep?
VLADIMIR. I don't know.
ESTRAGON (*after a pause*) Where shall we go?
VLADIMIR. Not far.
ESTRAGON. Oh, yes, let's go far away from here.
VLADIMIR. We can't.
ESTRAGON. Why not?
VLADIMIR. We have to come back tomorrow.
ESTRAGON. What for?
VLADIMIR. To wait for Godot.
ESTRAGON. Ah! (*He pauses*) He didn't come?

See p. 66.

VLADIMIR. No.

ESTRAGON. And now it's too late.

VLADIMIR. Yes, now it's night.

ESTRAGON. And if we dropped him? (*He pauses*) If we dropped him?

VLADIMIR. He'd punish us. (*He pauses and looks at the tree*) Everything's dead but the tree.

ESTRAGON (*moving R, turning and looking at the tree*) What is it?

VLADIMIR. It's the tree.

ESTRAGON. Yes, but what kind?

VLADIMIR. I don't know. A willow. (*He moves down C, turns and looks at the tree*)

weeping willow .

(ESTRAGON *moves up* C. *They both stand motionless gazing at the tree. There is a silence*)

ESTRAGON. Why don't we hang ourselves?

VLADIMIR. With what?

ESTRAGON. You haven't got a bit of rope?

VLADIMIR. No.

ESTRAGON. Then we can't.

VLADIMIR. Let's go.

ESTRAGON (*moving to R of Vladimir*) Wait, there's my belt.

VLADIMIR. It's too short.

ESTRAGON. You could hang on to my legs.

VLADIMIR. And who'd hang on to mine?

ESTRAGON. True.

VLADIMIR. Show all the same.

(ESTRAGON *loosens the cord that holds up his trousers which, much too big for him, fall about his ankles. They look at the cord*)

That might do at a pinch. But is it strong enough?

ESTRAGON. We'll soon see. Here.

(*They each take an end of the cord and pull. It breaks. They almost fall*)

stage action? comedy!

VLADIMIR. Not worth a curse.

ESTRAGON (*after a pause*) You say we have to come back to-morrow?

VLADIMIR. Yes.

ESTRAGON. Then we can bring a good bit of rope.

VLADIMIR. Yes.

ESTRAGON (*after a pause*) Didi.

VLADIMIR. Yes.

ESTRAGON. I can't go on like this.

VLADIMIR. That's what you think.

ESTRAGON. If we parted? That might be better for us.

VLADIMIR. We'll hang ourselves tomorrow. (*He pauses*) Unless Godot comes.

but of course he never will.

ESTRAGON. And if he comes?

VLADIMIR. We'll be saved. (*He removes his hat, peers inside it, feels about inside it, shakes it, knocks on the crown, and replaces it on his head*)

ESTRAGON. Well? Shall we go?

VLADIMIR. Pull on your trousers.

ESTRAGON. What?

VLADIMIR. Pull on your trousers.

ESTRAGON. You want me to pull off my trousers?

VLADIMIR. Pull *on* your trousers.

ESTRAGON (*realizing his trousers are down*) True. (*He pulls up his trousers*)

(*There is a silence*)

VLADIMIR (*presently*) Well? Shall we go?

ESTRAGON. Yes, let's go.

They do not move. There is a pause, then—

the CURTAIN *quickly falls*

FURNITURE AND PROPERTY LIST

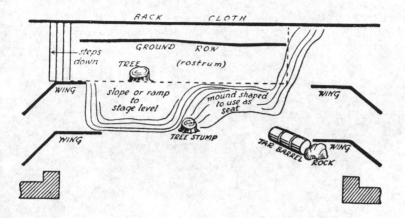

ACT I

On stage: Tar barrel
                Stump
                Tree (without leaves)

Off stage: Heavy bag (Lucky)
                Folding stool (Lucky)
                Pozzo's coat (Lucky)
                Picnic basket. *In it:* piece of chicken, piece of bread, bottle of
                      wine (Lucky)
                Rope (Pozzo)
                Whip (Pozzo)

Personal: VLADIMIR: turnips, carrot, and rubbish in pockets, bowler hat
                POZZO: spectacles, watch, pipe, box of matches, vaporizer,
                      handkerchief, pouch with tobacco, bowler hat
                ESTRAGON: bowler hat
                LUCKY: bowler hat

ACT II

Set: Leaves on tree
        Lucky's hat RC
        Boots down C

Off stage: Whip and rope (Pozzo)
Basket, bag and stool (Lucky)

Personal: Vladimir: string, radish
Lucky: hat
Estragon: thin string as belt

LIGHTING PLOT

Property fittings required: none

Exterior. A road. The same scene throughout
THE MAIN ACTING AREAS are at a mound C, RC and at a barrel LC

ACT I.   Early evening
To open: Effect of sunset

Cue 1   The sun sets suddenly   (Page 37)
          Reduce general lighting

Cue 2   The moon rises   (Page 37)
          Bring in moonlight effect

ACT II. Early evening
To open: Effect of sunset

Cue 3   The sun sets suddenly   (Page 68)
          Reduce general lighting

Cue 4   The moon rises   (Page 68)
          Bring in moonlight effect

MADE AND PRINTED IN GREAT BRITAIN BY
LATIMER TREND & COMPANY LTD PLYMOUTH

MADE IN ENGLAND